New Woodturning

Techniques and Projects

Schiffer Publishing Ltd®

4880 Lower Valley Road • Atglen, PA 19310

Advanced
Level

New Woodturning
Techniques and Projects

Helga Becker | Photography by Richard Becker

Other Schiffer Books on Related Subjects:

Wood Art Today: Furniture, Vessels, Sculpture, Dona Z. Meilach, ISBN 978-0-7643-1912-9
Home Woodworker Series: 14 Wooden Boxes You Can Make, Jim Harrold, ISBN 978-0-7643-4243-1
Direct Wood Sculpture: Technique, Innovation, Creativity, Milt Liebson, ISBN 978-0-7643-1299-1

Library of Congress Control Number: 2016943602

Originally published as *Neues drechseln für Fortgeschrittene* by Haupt Verlag AG, Bern © 2010 Haupt Verlag AG. Translated from the German by Jonee Tiedemann.

Designed by die-design-wiese.de, Bollschweil, Germany
Cover design by Matt Goodman
Photography by Richard Becker, Steinheim, Germany
Technical review by Sean McKnight
Type set in Frutiger Lt Std

ISBN: 978-0-7643-5018-4
Printed in China

Published by Schiffer Publishing, Ltd.
4880 Lower Valley Road
Atglen, PA 19310
Phone: (610) 593-1777; Fax: (610) 593-2002
E-mail: Info@schifferbooks.com
Web: www.schifferbooks.com

For our complete selection of fine books on this and related subjects, please visit our website at www.schifferbooks.com. You may also write for a free catalog.

Schiffer Publishing's titles are available at special discounts for bulk purchases for sales promotions or premiums. Special editions, including personalized covers, corporate imprints, and excerpts, can be created in large quantities for special needs. For more information, contact the publisher.

We are always looking for people to write books on new and related subjects. If you have an idea for a book, please contact us at proposals@schifferbooks.com.

CONTENTS

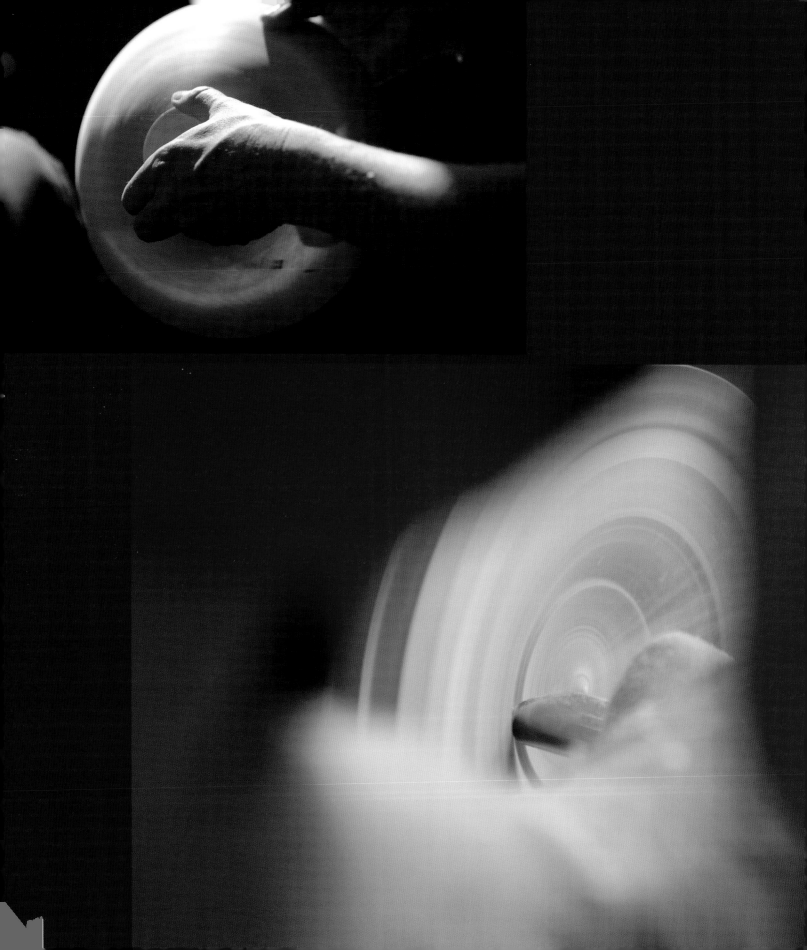

PREFACE

Any woodturner who's become familiar with the basic techniques will confirm what comes next: a desire to work with larger, more challenging dimensions and to learn new and more difficult techniques. In my courses and workshops, which are dedicated to different turning techniques, projects, or specific tools, I'm often called on to address the challenges that these advanced experiments raise for less-experienced woodturners, as well as for experienced turners.

I wrote this book to help you successfully handle these challenges, without endangering the project's well-being or your own. My husband, Richard Becker, provided the photographs, which play an important role here. They illustrate the individual steps from the perspective of the woodturner, and show important details relating to the handling of your equipment, the various options for clamping, the use of special tools, and so on.

The book begins with nine woodturning projects of my own design. For the next nine projects, I invited five colleagues who have dealt extensively with the relevant techniques and have even developed special clamping solutions. These internationally-renowned woodturning artists visited my workshop to demonstrate the making of their projects. I am immensely grateful to them.

The projects involve ten modern and traditional woodturning techniques that can be applied to create both contemporary pieces and traditional artistic pieces. These techniques, as you'll see, can result in sculptural figures, bowls, decorative objects, hats, canisters, lamps. . . .

The detailed, step-by-step instructions allow the projects to be made even by hobby woodturners who haven't yet accumulated that much experience with advanced techniques. However—and this is important—basic knowledge about techniques and about how to handle tools are prerequisites.

In the photo gallery at the end of the book, the woodturners share pieces that will inspire you to master the technical aspects and develop appealing designs for your own projects. Enjoy this book, and especially, enjoy your turning.

Note:
At the advanced level, the importance of precision in your woodturning is even more obvious and essential.
The measurements given throughout the book are in metric, not standard, for that reason.

ABOUT THE TURNERS

HELGA BECKER

I am a trained woodturner and have been running my own woodturning shop since 2000 (Neue Drechslerei), where I offer courses for beginners and advanced students. As one of the few woman woodturners, I have been invited to lead workshops and courses at international symposiums and have been able to travel extensively, including to Norway, England, France, Switzerland, and the United States.

My pieces are based on contemporary designs and combine traditional woodturning techniques and the natural qualities of the wood with the aspiration to fit into a modern, living environment. My works are sold in galleries and design shops.

Since 2004, I have also been active as an author. Together with my husband, the photographer, Richard Becker, I have published books about woodturning and I write for various national and international woodturning magazines.

If you still have questions regarding turning techniques or the design of the pieces after reading this book, you may contact me via www.helga-becker.de.

RICHARD BECKER

My husband, Richard Becker, has trained and worked as a photographer specializing in furniture and advertising, and in recent years his work has focused on architecture, interior design, theater, and journalism. His work is published in books and magazines. For more information, visit www.becker-fotografie.de.

Since our first joint book project, we have published four books together about woodturning. In this book, Richard's photographs enable you to re-create the projects step by step. Large-format photos and detail shots are helpful in clearly showing you difficult processes or the correct use of tools.

The beautiful photographs in the gallery section, highlighting the finished pieces, are intended to inspire you to make your own creations.

ELI AVISERA

I first met Eli in 2003, during a meeting of woodturners in Puy Saint Martin, in France. He is a very skilled craftsman who relishes his work, and he has created his own workshop in Jerusalem, where he teaches the many topics related to carpentry, woodturning, and carving. For many years he has been a most welcome guest at events related to the woodturning scene. He has traveled to many countries and delighted audiences with his demonstrations, in the United States, Japan, and France in particular. Since 2008, Eli has also been active in my woodturning shop as a guest lecturer. He focuses on modern design. His calm and patient personality has resulted in his being an excellent teacher.

CHRISTIAN DELHON

Christian is French with roots in Switzerland, and is very level-headed and calm. The first time I met him was in the workshop of Jean-François Escoulen. While working, he is always humming a song or tapping the rhythm of a melody that nobody else can hear. This inner composure must be the reason he is capable of dealing with complex techniques of traditional artistic woodturners—the more difficult, the better. Christian loves to re-create historic woodturning pieces that he finds in old books or museums. But his own creations are also reminiscent of the old masters he admires. Christian is often invited to woodturning symposiums and travels extensively in the United States, Spain, and Ireland. Since 2004, Buddy, as his friends and colleagues call him, has been teaching at my workshop, and instructing learners in the Chinese sphere and the star-in-a-sphere designs.

JEAN-FRANÇOIS ESCOULEN

Jean-François was one of the first globetrotters of the woodturning scene I came to know. We met in Austria, in 2001, and have maintained a warm relationship ever since. Jeannot is a kind and funny person and a highly gifted woodturner. I have rarely met someone who is this confident, nimble, and quick with the tools. He comes from commercial woodturning but has left the conventions of restrictive traditional shaping behind, by pursuing eccentric woodturning intensively. To make his designs he had to develop special chucks that today are sold all over the world. Jeannot can be found at events and courses held all over the world, and so I am particularly happy about the fact that he still finds the time to teach at my workshop.

ROLAND WALTER

After completing a course with the Father of Hat Turning, Johannes Michelsen, at my workshop, Roland dedicated himself to the woodturning of hats as well. I have observed him ever since doing this work, and I am happy that he is now offering courses on the topic at my workshop. As a trained carpenter, Roland knows a lot about wood and its manipulation and processing. He has a wealth of tips and tricks regarding the treatment of freshly cut wood that he uses for his hat creations. In terms of shape and comfort, they are at least as good as hats made from leather or felt.

JO WINTER

I met Jo (Joachim) during one of the open-house events at my workshop. He discovered woodturning two decades ago, but only a few years ago he was able to convert his hobby into his profession and his calling. His pieces often include the flying shadow, which results when non-round parts are spun around a rotating axis; it usually looks like a light gray area, while the solid (round) wood is somewhat darker. His extensive experience has helped Jo to develop tools that make it possible to manufacture his pieces, which often require working at significant depths or in restricted spaces. Jo also offers courses at my workshop, Neue Drechslerei.

EQUIPMENT

The Workshop

I presume that you, the reader, already have some experience with woodturning and that you're familiar with the appropriate equipment for a woodturning workshop, or have set one up already. So I will just briefly outline the general features of a well-equipped workshop:

- Plenty of natural light from large windows, with the lathe positioned in front of them.
- Additional glare-free artificial lighting next to the lathe.
- Light-colored, smooth walls to improve the light and to keep dust from adhering.
- Sufficient space around the lathe to provide unrestricted access and movement for the woodturner, even when using (often rather long) tools; and with tools and accessories nearby that work space, on the walls or inside cabinets and carts.
- A slip-free and warm floor surface.
- Enough electrical outlets for the lathe, lighting system, and accessories.
- A powerful suction system for removing shavings directly at the lathe and, if possible, including an air filter.
- A heating system, so the workshop can be used year-round.
- A furnace for the filings and shavings is very convenient, too.
- Enough space for additional handy equipment such as a bench grinder, a drill press, and a workbench or table.
- A band saw should also be part of your tool kit. However, it can be located in another room or covered space.

The Lathe

For basic techniques and working with smaller pieces, bench lathes or medium-sized machines with their own support frame are fine. However, more advanced techniques require a more professional lathe. We can outline the advantages of these machines by using the high-quality lathe Oneway 2436 (see photo on opposite page) as our example.

The first important factor to consider for a lathe is its weight. For large pieces or eccentric work it should not be less than 440 pounds (200 kg). A weight of around 550 pounds (250 kg) would be even better. Anything above this weight improves stability and smooth operation, for example, when working with large wetwood blanks, burl, trunk sections with bark, or eccentrically-clamped workpieces. The drum-shaped body of the Oneway 2436 absorbs vibrations very well, particularly when the tube is filled with sand. (Some woodturners have even filled it with cement for extremely large pieces.) Other lathes are fitted with a cast base with braces and a frame consisting of heavy material that provides stability.

A maximum height of about 9¾ inches (25 cm) should be standard for high-quality lathes. Our example lathe has a maximum height of 11⅞ inches (30 cm) over the base, allowing for a turning diameter of almost 23⅝ inches (60 cm)! Using an exterior turning device, this size can be increased significantly. Other top-of-the-line lathes allow you to increase the turning diameter via a rotary headstock. Both types allow for working ergonomically in the appropriate position.

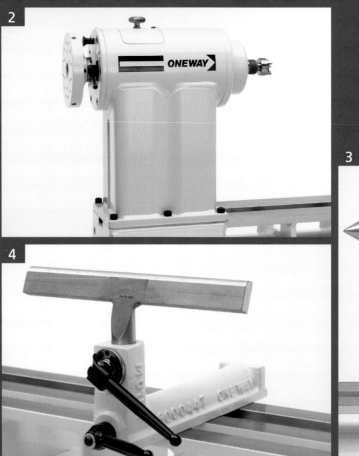

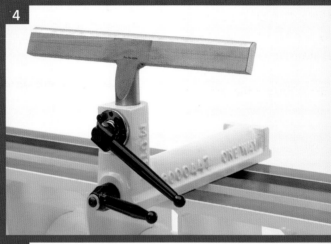

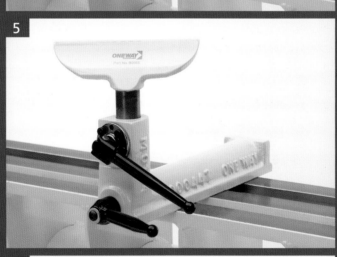

1__Electronics

An especially valuable improvement in modern lathes is the electronic speed control. While traditional commercial woodturning usually involves working between the tips with three or four speeds being adequate, the projects and turning techniques of amateur and professional woodturners have changed quite a lot during the past twenty-five years. Large bowls and vases made from heavy and wet or moist wood or burl require extremely slow initial speeds due to the considerable imbalance. The same applies to eccentrically or multi-axis turned pieces. The continuously variable electronic setting allows for adjusting the speed to the requirements of the piece (low initial speed) and for increasing the speed as work progresses. The continuously variable speed settings usually offer speeds between 50 and 3,300 rpm.

2__Headstock

In high-quality lathes the spindle head and the tailstock are usually made from gray cast iron to contribute stability. When purchasing a lathe, make sure that the spindle features two bearings, which are separated from each other. A spindle thread size of M33 x 3.5 allows for fitting chucks or faceplates from various manufacturers. A spindle with a cone seat (usually MT2 or MT3) allows for fitting drivers of various diameters. Good lathes also feature a holding fixture at the spindle. This allows for setting the spindle at several positions. A holding fixture also lets you divide the circumference of the work piece into even sections, for drilling, milled profiles, structures, and so on.

3__Tailstock

The tailstock should have a barrel stroke of $3\frac{1}{8}$ to $3\frac{15}{16}$ inches (80 to 100 mm). A precision ruler on the barrel, such as the one featured on the Oneway 2436, allows for precise drilling on the lathe. Obviously, the tips of the driver and the rotating tip should meet at the center of the axis at any of the tailstock's positions to allow for precise work.

4__5__Tool Rest

The tool rest and its support must glide smoothly on the base and be able to be adjusted and locked with one hand. Locking levers facilitate this job significantly, and are certainly preferred over threaded versions. You should invest in at least two tool rests of different widths. This allows for placing a short tool rest very close to the work piece for small pieces. With longer work pieces you save yourself the task of constantly moving the tool rest due to the increased reach of the long version.

Good lathes also feature a variety of practical accessories. The most important ones are multi-jaw chucks and faceplates:

6__Faceplates

When buying faceplates, consider their material as well as the diameter of the plate. I've found from experience that aluminum faceplates tend to be unstable. The material tends to give with large weights. This makes precise work impossible and means that safe operation is no longer guaranteed. Faceplates made from gray cast iron or steel are superior. They remain firm even with large weights and allow for safe fastening of the blank.

6__Four-Jaw Chuck

The various manufacturers of lathes produce their own lathe chucks. For example, the Oneway company has developed lathe chucks of various sizes that

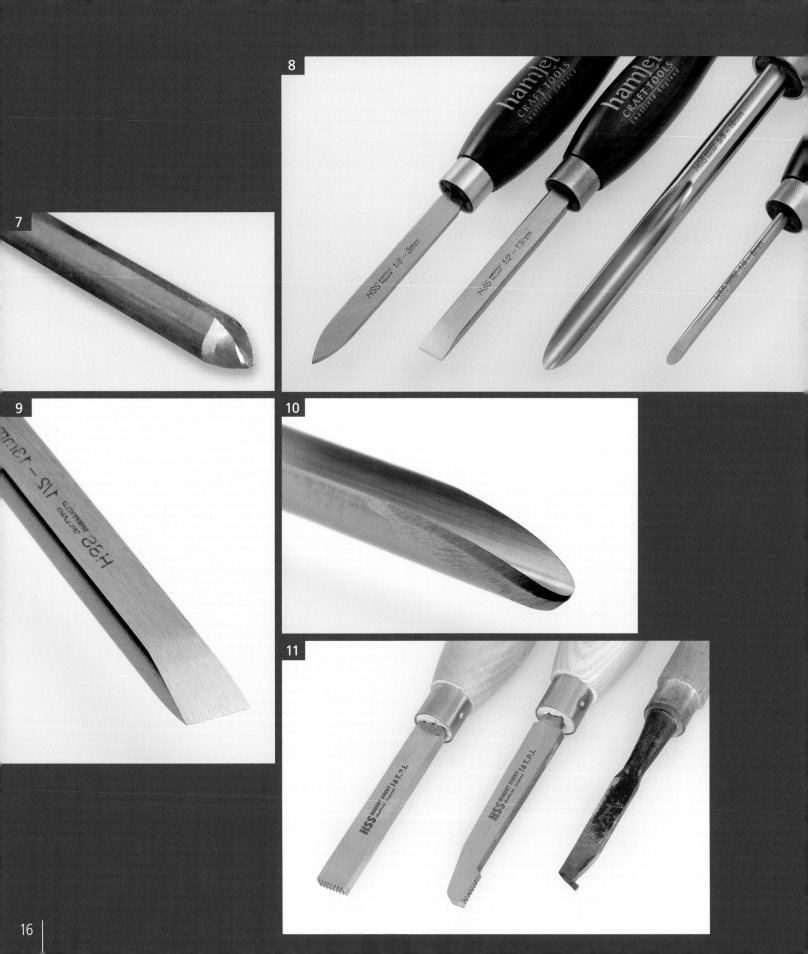

7

8

9

10

11

16

perfectly match the features and capacities of their lathes. Accessories include clamps and jaws of various diameters and heights, faceplate segments, drivers, and screws.

The base sections are fitted to the relevant lathes (including those of other manufacturers) with precision adapters of varying thread sizes. And special threading can be cut precisely into adapters consisting of solid material (without threads). When purchasing a lathe chuck, make sure it is firm and stable, check whether a good range of accessories is available, and make sure that the chuck can be easily fitted to a different (new) lathe if necessary, for example when switching from a smaller to a larger lathe.

The Tools

We won't discuss the details of basic tools—roughing gouges, cropping steel and other gouges, oval skew chisels—here. Their applications and handling are covered in basic woodturning courses, and should be familiar to you before making these projects. Here are the special tools that are used in the projects in this book:

7__Gouge with Crowned and Double Bezel

For his hat project, Roland Walter used a chisel made by Oneway with a wide, V-shaped groove that he grinds in his own special way. The crowned and sharpened large bezel provides a good support surface when approaching the wood. This is particularly helpful when working with extremely thin walls like those that result from turning hats. The second bezel, narrow and very sharp, provides an excellent surface finish.

8__Avisera Tools

Eli Avisera has modified a large number of traditional tools and adapted them to the requirements of his own work and the new applications of modern woodturning.

9__ Eli has fitted parting tools, broader parting tools used primarily by French woodturners, and chisels with a crowned (convex) bezel. The tool can be carefully rolled on the rounded surface until the blade reaches the wood. The depth of the cut and therefore the size of the shaving can be sensed and controlled by beginners as well.

10__ The Avisera bowl gouge features a deep and very tight concavity. Hence the material at the flanks remains fairly strong and firm. Usually fitted with a deep lateral downward bezel, the blade is initiated by a second narrow bezel. This results in the blade being thinner and very sharp. It assures a perfect surface finish. This second bezel is also used with Eli's spindle gouge. The profiles of these tubes, however, are flatter. They are particularly suitable for working with end grain wood.

11__Thread and Groove Making

A detailed description of the tools can be found on page 83.

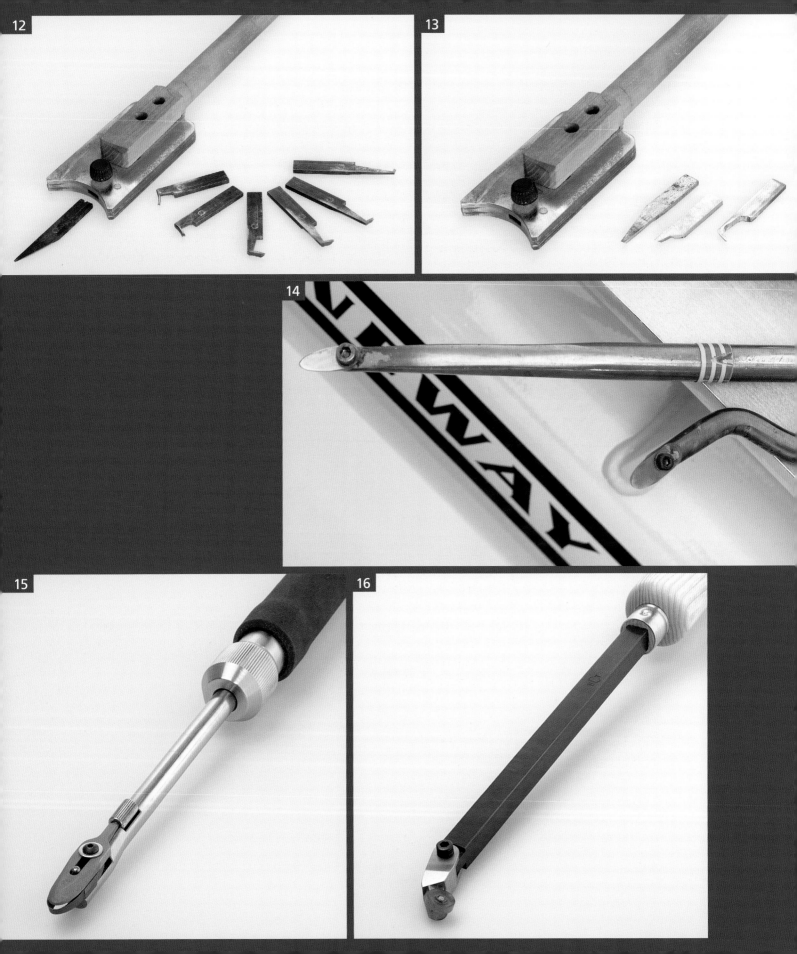

Delhon Tools

Christian Delhon has spent much time and effort in the creation of Chinese spheres and star-in-sphere pieces. He has developed special tools for these techniques, which he has also started to sell commercially.

12__Tool Kit for Chinese Spheres

The HSS cutting tools are affixed to a custom-made mounting and guided on a horizontal base table (see photo on page 127). The tool kits are available with five blades (for five spheres inside of each other) and with seven blades (for seven spheres inside of each other).

13__Tool Kit for Star in Sphere

For this project, three different parting tools are affixed to a special mounting and guided on the horizontal base. Both tool kits are used together with a special spherical chuck, also developed by Christian; it is described on page 119.

14__Jo Winter Tools

Jo Winter's special tools often leave standing, edgy surfaces which, while rotating, are visible only as shadows. Also, some of his creations consist of multi-axially-turned projects, where the areas that are not in line with the turning axis can only be perceived as shadows. The tools for these projects must be able to be used in constricted spaces without the possibility of much movement, and must not collide with the shadow surfaces. Jo has developed cutting plates of several sizes and shapes, as well as shafts and handles. Both of our projects feature his woodpecker's beak, a small and efficient HSS blade. It can be oriented vertically or swiveled to the left or right. Fitted with either a straight or a curved shaft, the tool allows for reaching great depths or hidden angles, even within constricted spaces.

15__Exocet

This tool is particularly suited for medium to large end-grain pieces. Because of the covered blade, the tool will not become stuck. The twin HSS blade is easy to sharpen with a diamond file. The shaft, with an eccentric mechanism in the handle, can be held so as to provide the optimal cutting depth. The Exocet tool is particularly handy for working large pieces or those where the work area is difficult to see due to a small opening. It allows beginners to gradually become more confident in working with end-grain woods and greater depths.

16__BCT

The BCT (Bierton Craft Tool) is a further development of the traditional ring tool. Because of its closed surface, it can be better controlled than an open ring. The hollow groove that is cut into the surface provides a superb finish, since the blade does not scrape, but instead it cuts. The square shaft stabilizes the tool, even at great depths. Its side arm can be swiveled to the left, and is therefore suitable for relief-turned shapes of end-grain wood. The sharp cutting wheel makes for excellent surface finishes. With this tool, clearing out material takes somewhat longer, as the relatively small cutting wheel cannot remove a lot of material at a time. Nevertheless, I use it quite a lot, for example, with small pieces that require less removal of wood or when, after having cleared out material with larger pieces using a tool such as the Exocet, I want to improve the surface quality or create a very thin wall.

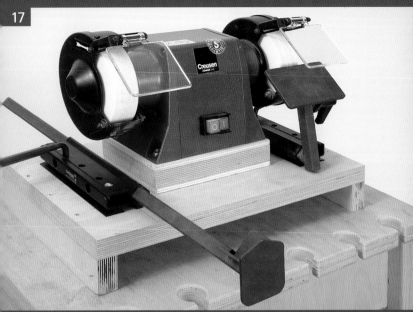

Sharpening Devices for Woodturning Tools

Generally, whetting (sharpening) the tools used in this book doesn't require any unusual sharpening devices or accessories. A basic sharpening kit should be part of your equipment.

17__Grinding Station

This is where craftsmen are divided into those favoring dry or wet sharpening methods.

In wet grinding, the disc slowly rotates in a water bath. This provides for constant cooling of the disc, and the tool will not overheat. This method is very gentle with the material and particularly suitable for high-quality tools, such as those used for carving. The disadvantage is the slow speed, particularly when tools have to be resharpened. In addition, the water must be removed from the container after each application to keep the standing disk from soaking up water where it touches the water. When the grinding block is used again, the disc is not round anymore. It wobbles and makes it impossible to sharpen the tools with precision. Also, dust and dirt accumulate in the water and cover the disc, clogging the grinding surface.

In dry grinding, the tools are worked on the disc only, without water for cooling. The following points are important to take into account: the grinding disc should not turn at high speed. Between 1,000 and 1,500 rpm is best. Make sure the machine is fitted with a carborundum disc. The harder the steel, the softer the disc. The diameter of the grinding discs is also important. The larger the diameter of the grinding discs, the smaller the hollow grinding at the tool bezel. In other words, you should not allow the disc to grind down too much. Once the diameter of the disc falls below $5\frac{1}{8}$ to $5\frac{1}{2}$ inches (13 to 14 cm), the hollow grinding becomes rather prominent. The blade becomes more delicate, it becomes blunt more quickly, and it must be sharpened more often. Make sure you even out the disc on a regular basis, to smooth the resulting grooves and to create a flat disc surface.

You might notice that I tend toward the camp of dry sharpening. Especially since the sharpening process can be shortened by applying the appropriate implements, so the short grinding time prevents the tools from becoming too hot. The grinding accessories also have the advantage of providing the correct shape of the blade without leaving facets on the bezels. The Wolverine system of grinding accessories has proven to be an excellent choice in my workshop:

18__Grinding Jig

The Wolverine system is both simple and good. The basic kit includes a movable rod or grinding table. The tubes are inserted into a V-shaped groove of the rod. By moving the rod, the angle of the bezel can be copied or, if required, enlarged or scaled down. When mounting the Wolverine system, make sure that the supports are located at an adequate distance from the center of the grinding discs, about $6\frac{5}{16}$ inches (16 cm).

19__This will provide appropriate bezel angles. The grinding table provided with the basic kit can be adjusted in its distance from the grinding disc as well as with respect to its angle. Chisels, scrapers, or knives can be sharpened.

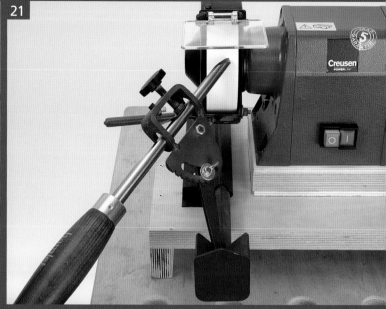

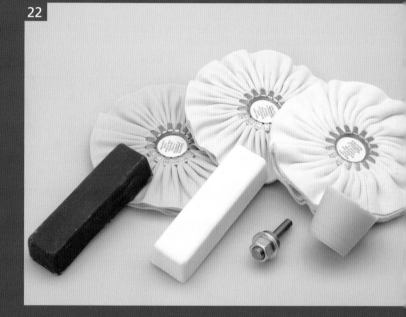

20__Grinding Accessory for the Skews

Basically, skew chisels can be sharpened using the table of the basic kit. However, I have seen, time and again, that untrained people are able to correctly copy the angle of the bezels, but they have difficulty maintaining the angle of the blade. This usually happens when the skew is sharpened manually. The problem is easily solved by using the skew grind, a grinding accessory. This extension is affixed perpendicularly into the rod of the basic kit. The skew is placed into the outer V-shaped grooves of the skew grind, so that the bezel lies on the grinding disc and the blade is oriented horizontally. When changing position (from one groove to the other) the tool is turned, so that the other bezel now touches the disc. This assures the same bezel angle on both sides, while the angle of the blade is also maintained.

21__Grinding Accessory for the Gouges

The fingernail grind can't be resharpened with the rod of the basic kit alone. Apart from turning around its axis, a swiveling movement at a specific angle is also required. The guide for the gouge is placed with its support leg into the rod of the basic kit and can be swiveled laterally. The angle of the support leg of the guide can also be adjusted. This allows for adjusting both the angle and the length of the laterally downward-facing bezel.

Tip: To re-create the same shape of the grind, the tool should be fixed so that it always sticks out with the same length over the support of the guide. For this purpose, I've made a mark next to the grinding block. For the various sizes of the bowl gouge, I have also added the appropriate angle marks directly onto the guide. This avoids searching for the right angle every time I have to grind.

The second small bezel, which is a feature of some of the previously mentioned special tools, can also be sharpened quickly and precisely.

Grinding Devices for Sanding

22__Sanding and Polishing Accessories

An outstanding sanding and polishing system for surface treatments is particularly suitable for small or asymmetrical pieces that are difficult to sand or polish on the lathe. The discs are fitted into the chuck or on a special spike, which is placed into the spindle. They are used successively with a special wax. The details can be found on page 125 with Project 12, Chinese Sphere.

You can save time and work more effectively by placing the three polishing discs next to each other onto a shaft (e.g., on a small, benchtop lathe). This way, the polishing system is always ready to be used and the three discs can be used consecutively, without having to mount and unmount the individual discs on the lathe.

23

24

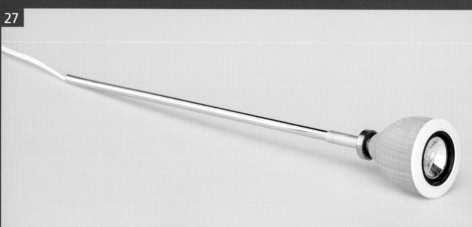

27

25

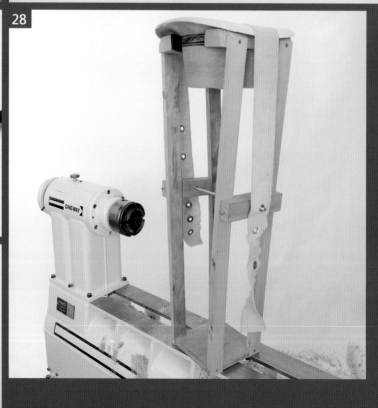

28

26

Additional Equipment

23 & 24__

Eccentric Chuck by Jean-François Escoulen

The third eccentric chuck developed by Jean-François is a significant improvement over chuck no. 2. As that is no longer in production, I want to focus on no. 3. This eccentric chuck features a bung, just like its two predecessors. However, not only can a spherical segment in the bung chuck be removed from the axis, the entire bung chuck can also be shifted parallel to the axis and turned around its own axis. Additionally, the chuck body itself can be adjusted. For this reason, the mounting thread for the spindle thread is also shaped as a spherical segment. The chuck body can be tilted laterally on this spherical segment. To keep the resulting imbalance under control, the left and right sides of the chuck feature weights, which can be adjusted so that the forces equalize each other.

You might be able to imagine some of the numerous possibilities offered by this chuck. However, to understand the full range of its applications, you need to do your own experiments.

Tip: Start out with only a few adjustments at a time, and with only slight shifts of the axis. Write down the individual changes so you can re-create them later. Keep in mind that by adjusting too often, the desired effects can neutralize each other.

25__Kirjes Sanding Accessories

This flexible system has proven to be very convenient. Sanding sleeves with grits of 50 to 400 can be fitted onto sanding rolls of different sizes. An air pump is used to inflate the sanding rolls to the desired firmness, to hold the sleeves in place. Part of the Kirjes system is a small yet powerful motor that moves a flexible shaft to which the sanding rolls are affixed. The shaft has a long and firm grip, which is great for narrow vessels and for working at great depths. A sanding roll cleaner allows for easy cleaning of the sanding sleeves and significantly prolongs their useful life.

Light Chuck

The final step, when turning hats, consists of working on the hat shelf. This surface should ideally be as thin as the side walls. However, since you cannot measure or sense this spot, Johannes Michelsen, the father of hat woodturning, invented the light chuck.

26__ A conical chuck body consisting of pressed wood is covered with neoprene or foam rubber. Hat blanks of various diameters can be securely affixed without getting pressure marks.

27__ This chuck body is illuminated; its lighting consists of a metal tube, cable, low-voltage lamp, and its socket, also of pressed wood. The cable is passed through the spindle via the metal tube and held in place with a simple clamp at the left exit of the spindle. The socket of the lamp is affixed inside the chuck body with a ball bearing. This keeps the lamp from turning with the lathe, while it is guided by the chuck. This light chuck can be used not only for hats, but for bowls or vases as well.

28__Bender

When turning hats we take advantage of the drying characteristics of wood. A cross-grain wood blank, which has been cut symmetrically to the core area, will usually warp into an even oval. To increase its fit and to give it more pizzazz—particularly the brim—a so-called bender can be utilized. It consists of a wooden frame into which the still-moist blank is fixed and shaped, with the help of rubber bands.

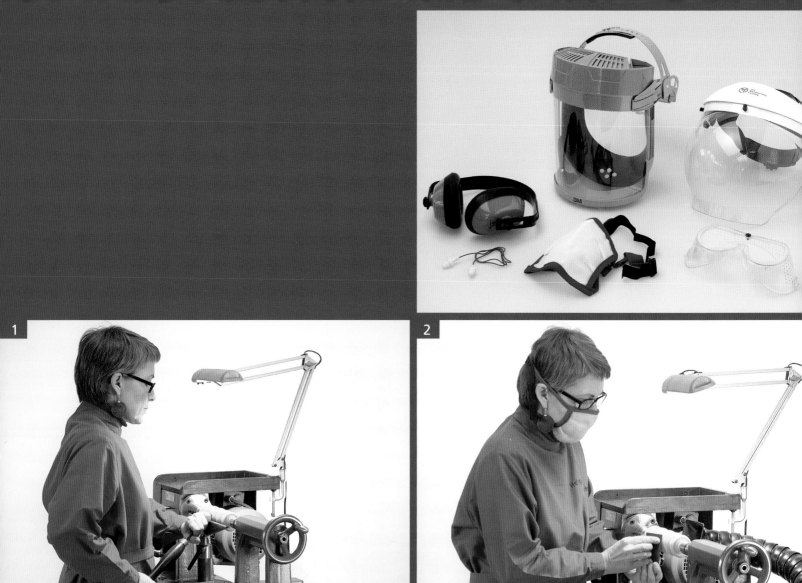

1

2

3

4

WORK SAFETY

Even when you work with great concentration and attention, accidents cannot be entirely ruled out. But the risk of injury while turning can be minimized by following these suggestions:

1__ Do not wear clothing with wide sleeves or loose parts. They might get caught on the spinning piece. Avoid sweaters or cardigans; their loops get caught by even the smallest chips and slivers. Many cotton and denim fabrics are appropriate. In the photos I'm wearing a jacket that's a modern interpretation of the traditional woodturning work coat. The coat is closed at the back with Velcro and two crossed straps. Wide flaps close the large pockets (front), while cuffs at the neck and wrists prevent chips from getting on the clothing.

2__ Remove any jewelry and watches, and tie back long hair. Vacuum the fine sanding dust directly at the lathe, and wear a respiratory mask, which protects the lungs from fine dust.

3__ Wear safety goggles or a face shield to protect your eyes and face from flying splinters, wood chips, or pieces of bark. Full-face visors with air filters are available. They provide protection for eyes, face, and lungs. But keep in mind that they are relatively heavy and uncomfortable to wear for extended periods of time. When working with a saw or a router, good hearing protection is indispensable.

4__ Firm, sturdy footwear provides secure footing at the machine and protects your feet from injuries caused by falling objects.

Before switching on the lathe, make sure the work piece has no cracks, which might be dangerous; that it is secured firmly; that the blank can turn freely past the tool rest; and that all of the moving parts (tool rest, support, tailstock, tail spindle, and headstock) are tight. Also, check the set speed before switching on the lathe and adjust it if necessary. If you are not entirely sure how fast the speed should be, let it run too slow rather than too fast. Once the lathe runs smoothly, you can increase the speed.

Machines with electronic speed-control should be used with this method, to find the optimal speed: Set the control to zero and place one hand on the base of the lathe. Turn on the machine with the other hand and slowly increase the speed. You will notice that there are speed regions where the vibrations are stronger or weaker. Choose a speed where the vibrations are as low as possible.

Always switch off the machine when adjusting the tool rest, and remove it when sanding.

Make sure you have good lighting in the workshop and at the lathe.

Remove shavings and dust on a regular basis. This makes for less dust and keeps the workshop accessible. Also, it keeps pests and mold spores from moist shavings from settling in the workshop. For the same reasons, you should ventilate the area regularly.

Work with great attention and take your time. If you are unable to concentrate, the risk of injury increases significantly.

Always follow the manufacturer's recommendations for operating the machines, and avoid taking unnecessary risks!

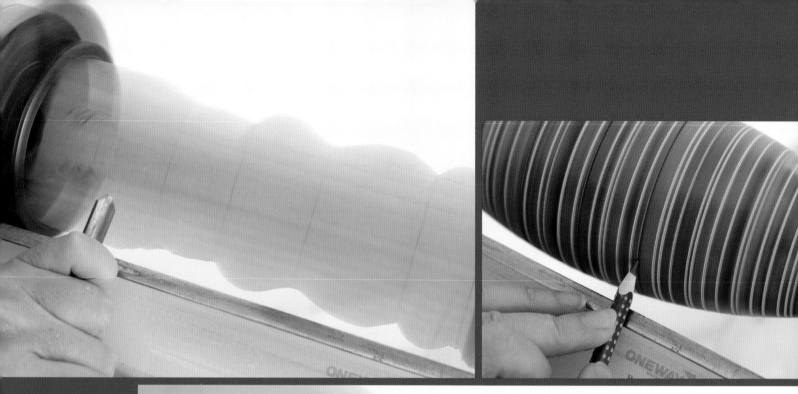

TURNING TECHNIQUES

Turning Spheres

In the first project, we'll explore turning spheres, which is regarded as the supreme discipline of woodturners. Making a sphere by hand requires precise workmanship, the correct manipulation of tools, and the knowledge of how to chuck and rechuck the blank to create a perfect sphere.

Angular Turning

Most of the pieces created on the lathe are rotated symmetrically. Angular turning allows you to expand the design possibilities to create different profiles: in one single piece, objects with planar sections, or open-work pieces.

Wet Turning of Cross-Grain Wood

Working with wet wood is enjoyable, because much less dust is created and freshly cut wood is (almost) always available. It allows for working larger pieces, since the moist wood hasn't formed cracks, unlike dried wood. If we consider the fact that wood bends after (or even during) the work process on the lathe, our design options become greater, in terms of avoiding the strict, rotational symmetry of the lathe.

Wet Turning of End-Grain Wood

Carving out bowls and vases from end-grain wood requires special tools. The correct cutting direction to get a clean surface is from the center toward the edge. So the tools must have certain characteristics that allow for this cutting direction. The tools that can be used and how to handle them are explained in two of the projects.

Thread Cutting

This technique allows you to cut a thread into two independent sections, so they can be joined firmly and opened again. Thus, thread-cutting is particularly handy for projects involving containers, but it can also be used for technical objects, like wooden clamping or supporting structures.

Turning Bowls

Once your tool-handling abilities are more advanced, you're able to work with more challenging shapes. The design aspect of the piece becomes more important, including looking beyond the lathe and toward the further processing of the piece. In this section of the projects, we'll discuss some suggestions and ideas for details, proportions, colors, structures, and so on.

Artistic Turning

Traditional artistic turning techniques, which have been developed and applied over the previous centuries, are still attractive to turners today. The woodturner can excel at creating filigree and other highly decorative pieces with precise, calm, and patient work.

Eccentric Turning

The boundaries of rotational symmetry can be overcome with eccentric or poly-axial turning. Special chucks considerably expand the possibilities, and provide a firm hold on the pieces.

Turning Hats

Hats made from wood are as lightweight as their felt or leather counterparts, and they feature eye-catching grain patterns or beautiful colors. They're also very comfortable to wear. This project will show you how to create them.

Shadow Turning

Whenever out-of-round pieces turn on a rotational axis, a lighter area around a darker, massive core is visible: the so-called flying shadow. It is also created when round parts are removed from the axis and processed further. It's important to understand how to tell which sections must be further processed (or which ones *can* be further processed), and which tools are appropriate.

PROJECTS

Curly birch
Dia. 8 cm

1___SPHERE

HELGA BECKER

Materials	
Tools	Roughing gouge, 19 mm
	Continental gouge, 8 mm
	Continental gouge, 12 mm
	Spindle gouge, 12 mm
	Parting tool, 3 mm
Wood	Curly birch trunk/branch section diameter ca. 10 cm, length 13 cm
	Spruce or basswood for spherical chuck 10 x 10 x 10 cm
Accessories	Calipers
	Ruler

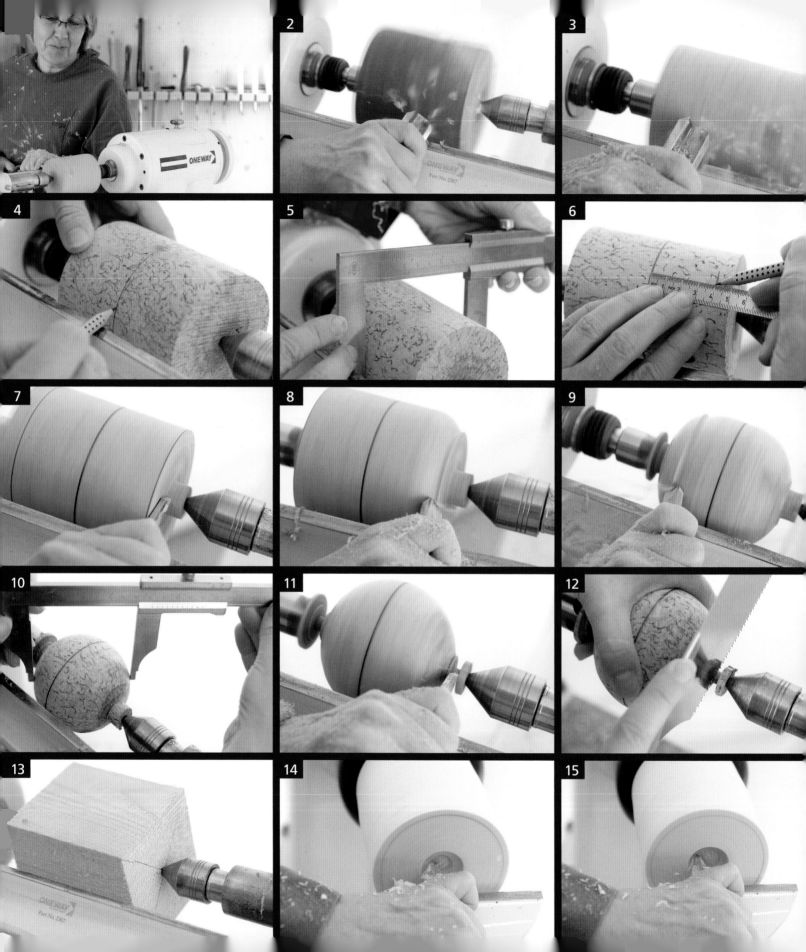

For the first project, I've chosen a particularly beautiful wood, natural curly birch. Curly birch features an expressive whorled grain. I've worked trunk sections into an entire series of spheres (see page 186).

1__Insert the trunk section between the centers and plane it off.

2__Due to its slow and whorled growth, the wood is very hard. Sharp tools are essential.

3__The blank is turned cylindrically to its maximum diameter. Small pieces of bark can remain visible; they make the finished sphere more interesting.

4__Mark the center of the cylinder, its equator, with a pencil and . . .

5__. . . use the calipers to measure the diameter at this location of the cylinder, which for this project is 8 cm.

6__From the center, transfer half of the measured diameter to each side, that is, 4 cm to the right and 4 cm to the left. This determines the position of the poles.

7__Using the parting tool, cut both sides back to a small stud (1 cm).

Tip: Make sure you cut perfectly vertical so that the diameter of the sphere at the poles won't become smaller or larger than at the equator.

8__Use the gouges to create the spherical shape.

Tip: Work in parallel on both sides. This allows for a better control of the symmetry. The center line must not be touched! It's important for rechucking later (see page 36, photo 17).

9__To achieve a clean surface it's important to place the bezel of the tool and to cut from the large to the small diameter.

10__The better your spherical shape at this stage, the easier it will be after rechucking. So keep controlling the distance (in this case, 8 cm) again and again by placing the calipers diagonally at different positions over the center line, or use a template.

Tip: It's better to leave extra material than to cut away too much. Excess material will be removed later when rechucking.

11__Once the spherical shape has been achieved, cut back the studs as much as possible . . .

12__. . . and saw them off.

13__Now chuck the spruce blank between the tips, plane it off, and add a stud to be clamped into the chuck.

14__After rechucking, hollow out with the spindle gouge so that the sphere blank can be fitted into this cavity to be processed further.

15__To do this, set the spindle gouge at the center and guide it toward the outside. When placing at the center, the tool is angled slightly toward the left.

Important: Don't set the tool horizontally! During the cut toward the outside, the gouge is also set farther to the left. This assures that only the highest section of the blade is cutting, and not the blade along its full length.

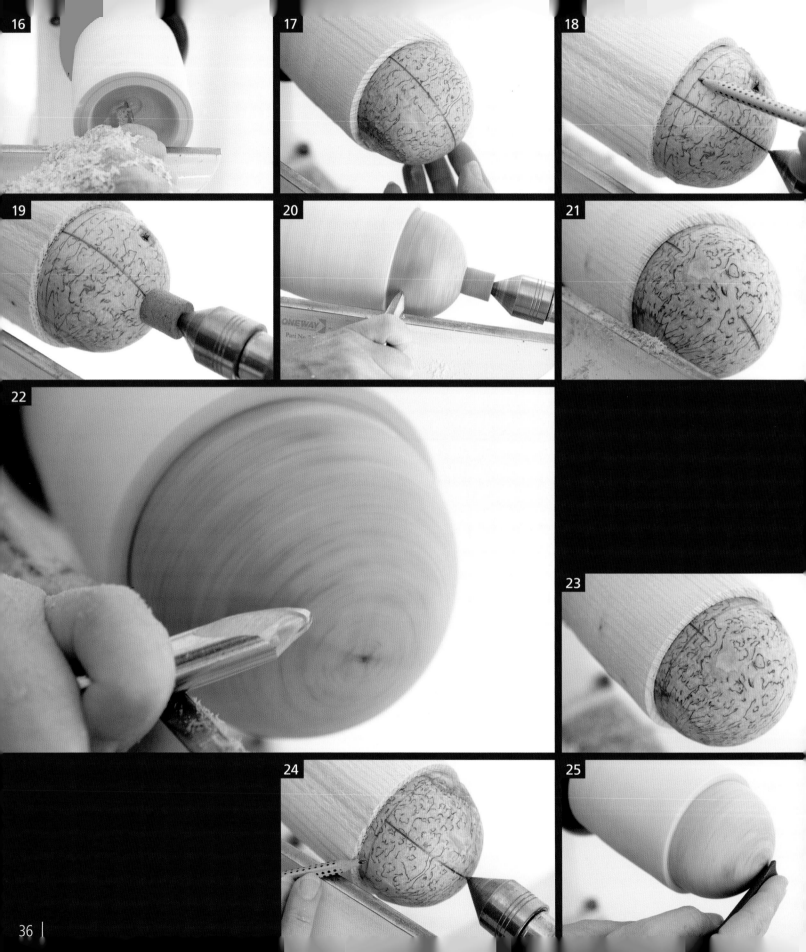

16__**Tip:** Use a flexible wood, such as spruce or basswood, for a spherical chuck. Make sure the wall is not too thick after hollowing out. A thin wall makes it easier to press the sphere into the chuck because the wall flexes and embraces the sphere. You might also want to slightly turn the cylinder from the outside. However, the wall shouldn't be too thin either, otherwise it might break out when pushing in the sphere. For this project it should be about 4 to 5 mm.

17__When hollowing out, keep checking the fit of the sphere. It should only fit into the spherical chuck about halfway or less. The studs must stay in front of the chuck. The sphere must fit well enough that it stays in place by itself.

Tip: If the hole in the spherical chuck turned out to be too deep, don't worry. The correct diameter of the opening is more important, because it determines the seat of the sphere. For the sphere to be held in front of the center of the spherical chuck, the diameter of the hole must be smaller than that of the diameter of the sphere! Don't get discouraged if it takes you a few attempts before the sphere is correctly placed.

18__Align the sphere so that the equator lies exactly on the axis. This can be done and controlled with the rotating tip. The centers of both poles must be equidistant to the edge of the spherical chuck and line up on the same axis. This line lies perpendicular to the first center line.

19__If the sphere is not yet firmly set into the spherical chuck or if you're still somewhat uncertain with the handling of the tools, you can secure the sphere with the rotating tip.

Tip: To avoid damage to the sphere, you should place a piece of felt or cork between the sphere and the tip.

20__First, rework the studs with small and delicate cuts until they have disappeared. To provide a spherical shape to the blank's free side, use the continental gouge to progress from the large to the small diameter. Remove only a little material with each cut and keep checking the shape regularly.

21__The exact spherical shape is obtained when the pencil marking of the original center line just about disappears. In other words, wherever you can still see the line you have to remove some material.

Important: Do not remove too much material per cut!

22__Finally, remove the rotating tip so you can work the center as well. A sharp spindle gouge can be used to remove the last bit from the center toward the edge.

Important: Apply only slight pressure!

23__Once the pencil marking is barely visible—or just barely invisible—this half of the sphere is done.

24__Now rechuck the sphere, and work the second half of the sphere the same way (the steps in photos 18 to 23).

25__When both halves have been finished, sand the sphere. It must be constantly rechucked in the spherical chuck and sanded briefly on all surfaces.

Important: Don't sand too much on any given spot or you might destroy the spherical shape!

Sand the sphere down to 400 grit, and then apply Danish oil to protect the surface and to emphasize the grain.

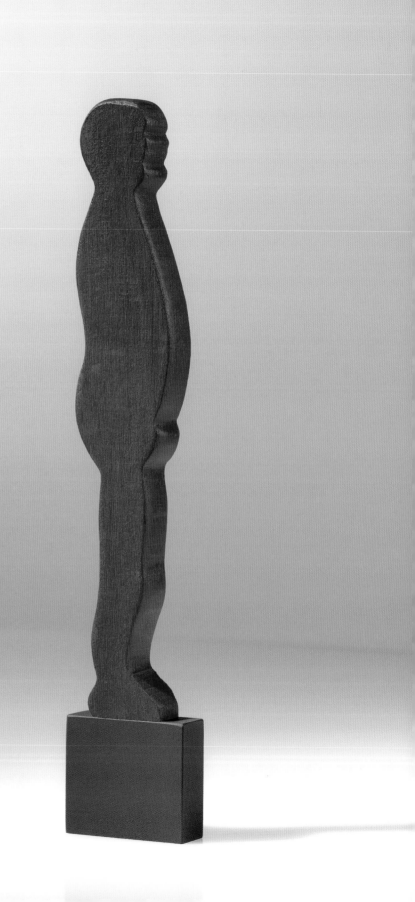

Beech
H 19 cm

2___HUMAN FIGURES

HELGA BECKER

Materials	
Tools	Continental gouge, 8 mm
	Continental gouge, 12 mm
	Spindle gouge, 12 mm
	Parting tool, 3 mm
Wood	2 pieces beech, each 3.5 x 1.3 x 25 cm **Important:** They should be planed and cut to length at 90 degrees!
Accessories	Strong packing tape

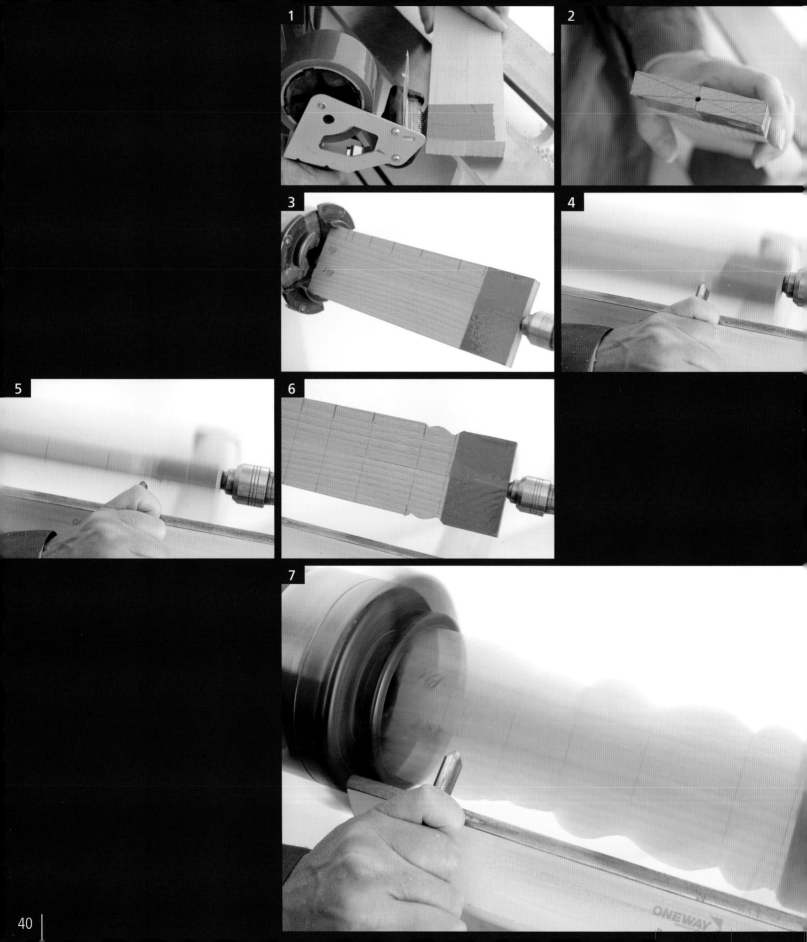

In this project, I've taken advantage of angular turning to design two different profiles in one piece. Just like in real life, my little humans feature six-pack bellies or potbellies, long or short legs, curved backs or straight shoulders. The result is girls, boys, women, men, grandpas, grannies, moms, dads . . . each one with its own character.

1__Tape the two pieces of beech together so that their narrow sides face each other. I have taped only one side here. However, for your safety, you should tape both sides.

2__Mark one long side diagonally and drill it at the center with a 5-mm bit.

3__Chuck both blanks so that the drilled face lies on the side of the rotating tip, which enters the drilled hole. The other side is inserted into the chuck.
Important: Make sure you use a pressure ring tip. While the tip enters the drill hole, it only centers the piece and doesn't exert any lateral pressure; but the pressure ring holds both wood pieces and keeps them together.

Mark the key profile edges on both sides of the wood pieces: head, torso, buttocks, thighs, knees, heels, etc. When the blank is rotating the pencil marks are visible.

4__Select the rotating speed so that the two pieces of wood aren't pushed apart—that is, not too fast. On the other hand, the angular surface needs to allow for easy work and for guiding the tool safely. So the speed shouldn't be too slow, either. I worked this piece at about 1,500 rpm.

5__Since you'll be working "in the shadow" at first—that is, the angular planes of the woods—you have to approach the wood carefully with your tool. The tool must be well-sharpened so that no pressure needs to be applied. Work with a fine and small shaving . . .

6__ . . . and check the result regularly. Make sure not to cut the profiles too deeply, since you'll be working the other side after rechucking.

7__During rotation the pencil marks are visible. You can use them to guide your profile design.

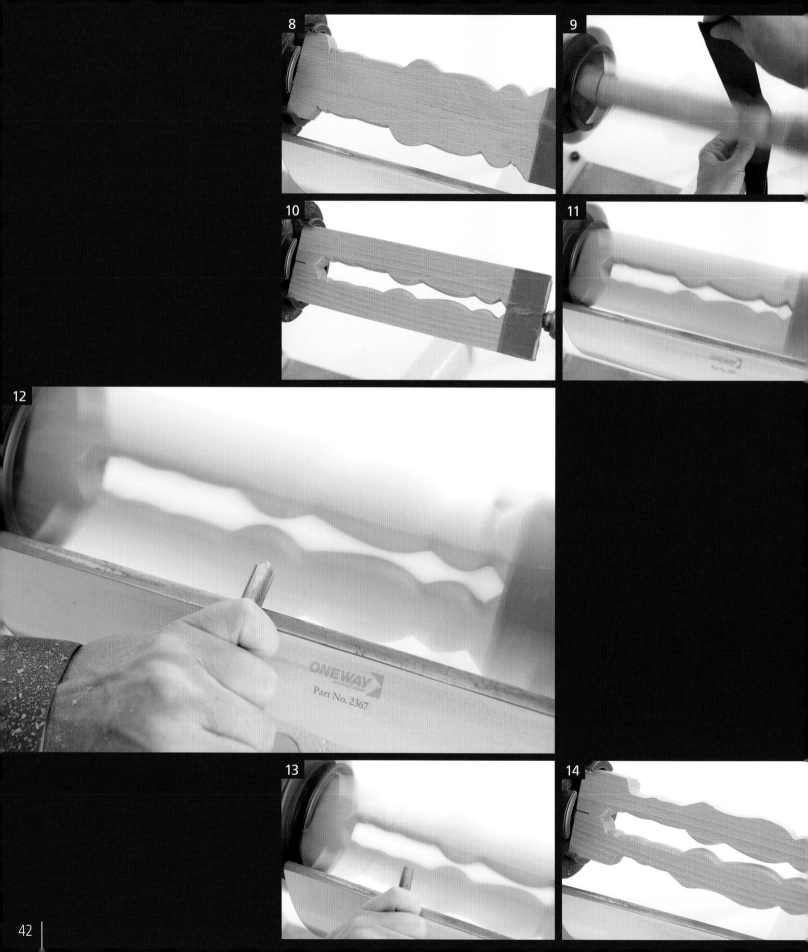

8__I've started with the back section. It's already clearly visible on both pieces of wood. Make sure you guide the tool properly to avoid grooves on the surface.
Tip: Use a firm and heavy tool.

9__To sand the profiles, use a long piece of abrasive paper held taut with both hands, and press it against the surface.
Important: Don't use your hand to press the paper onto the surface—you might hurt yourself!

10__After sanding, remove the piece from the chuck and take the packing tape off. Place the two wood pieces against each other so that the profiled sides lie inside, then tape them together again (on both sides if possible).

11__Once again, chuck the wood pieces between the chuck and the pressure ring tip. During rotation you can see the back profile of the two human figures at the inside.

12__You can now work the front side in relation to the back side. Approach the wood carefully with only slight pressure.

13__Keep checking whether the body parts correspond to each other correctly (shinbone at the height of the calves, knees at the back of the knee, etc.).

14__Both profiles are done now, and with one process we obtain two identical figures, thanks to the angular turning. The "belly profile" can now be turned. Then the rest of the wood on the head side of the twins is sawed off. At the feet it can be left on as a pedestal. For my piece I glued on different pedestals, which I colored gray (see the gallery, page 197).

As a different project, I attached some of these figures onto flexible metal rods of different heights, which I soldered to a heavy plate. That sculpture is standing in my yard. With a little wind, the figures sway softly back and forth; it's a beautiful sight!

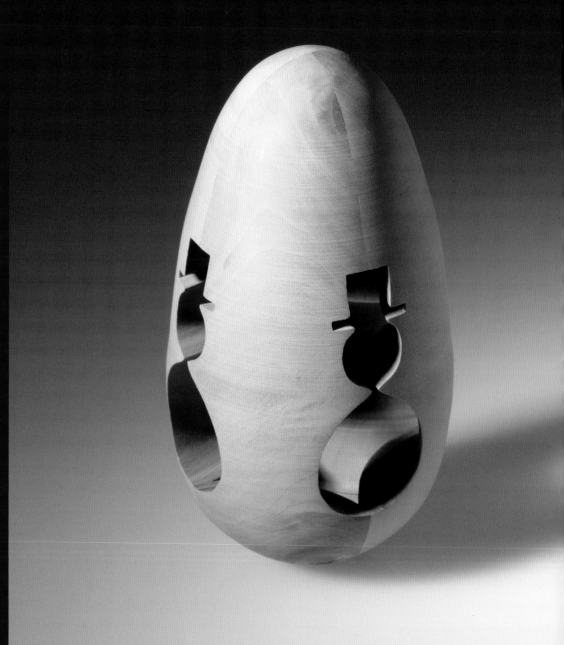

Pear
Dia. 6.5 cm
H 13.5 cm

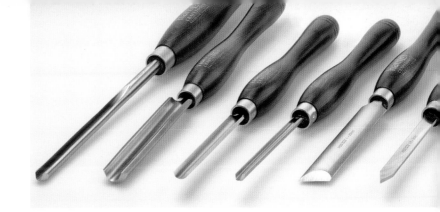

3___DECORATIVE SPHERE

HELGA BECKER

Materials		
Tools	Basic tools without a bowl gouge:	
	Roughing gouge, 19 mm	
	Continental gouge, 8 mm	
	Continental gouge, 12 mm	
	Parting tool, 3 mm	
	Oval skew chisel, 25 mm	
Wood	Pear, 7 x 7 x 18 cm	
	Important: The blank must be cut squarely and at right angles.	
Accessories	Cardboard	
	PVA glue	
	Clamps	

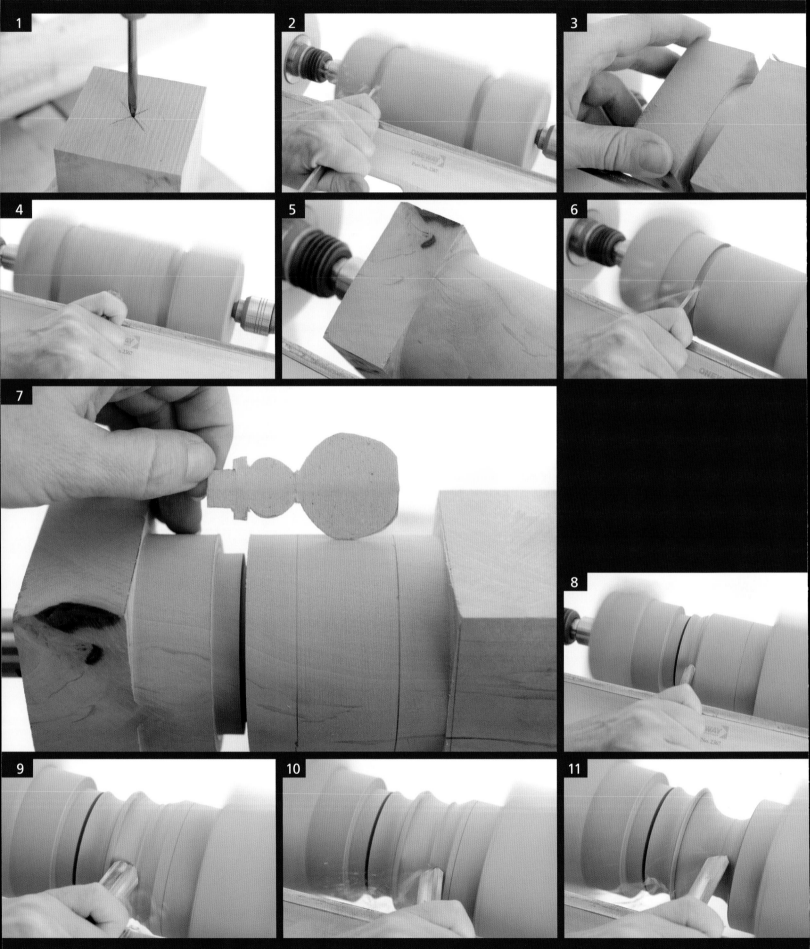

With the decorative sphere we increase the level of difficulty, by doing angular woodturning while at the same time working with four wood pieces that are then joined to form one single piece. Whether the pieces actually turn out to be spherical or more oval (more commonly the case) depends on the cut-out motif. Winter designs (like a snowman, tree, angel, or star) can adorn the Christmas tree. Other designs (a fish, airplane, house, etc.) are usable all year long. The important thing is that the motif needs to have a symmetrical outline.

1__Center the blank and center-punch it if necessary (prepunch a small hole in the center).

2__Place it between the centers; don't plane it, but instead, use the parting tool to mark the length of the surface where the motif will be placed.

3__Only perforate to the point of the blank's maximum diameter.

Important: Do not perforate any deeper!

4__Turn the entire surface between the perforations to this diameter.

5__**Important:** The radius must terminate with the surfaces of the square timber. The cylinder must be of the same size along its entire length, since this line will later form the symmetrical axis of the motif!

6__For the snowman the profile is now carved out into the depth, that is, "negatively."

Important: We have to create the negative profile so that the correct shape of the snowman appears later in the finished decorative sphere.

7__Start cutting off at the hat and work with the symmetrical axis (see photo 5) into the depth to obtain the corresponding size for the hat and brim.

8__Use the tube to turn the body of the snowman. Depending on the size of the profile, the 8-mm continental gouge (small snowball) . . .

9__ . . . or the 12-mm continental gouge (large snowball) is used.

10__For the deep grooves, always work from the large to the small diameter, that is, alternating between right to center and left to center. This will result in a smooth surface.

11__**Important:** Make sure the profiles aren't too deep! The maximum profile should be no more than a quarter of the total diameter of the blank, or problems may result later on (see page 49, photo 19).

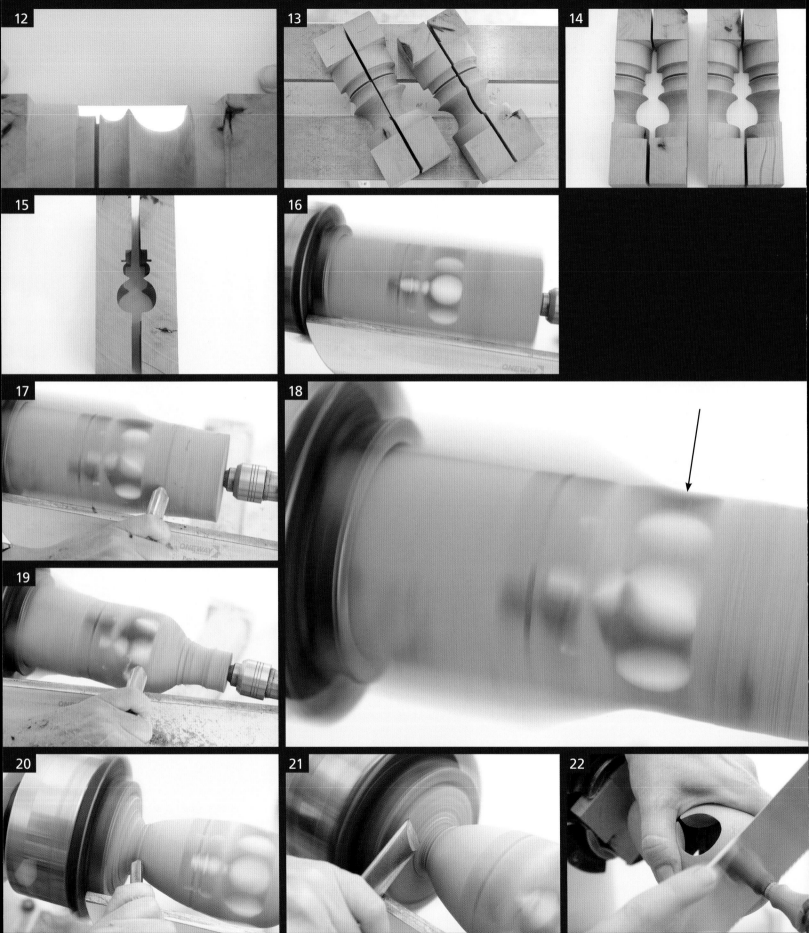

12__You can control the profile by placing a piece of paper or cardboard behind the blank so that the lower edge coincides with the symmetry axis. Then sand the finished profile.

Tip: Make sure not to sand down the fine edges.

13__Now unclamp the blank. Use a circular saw to cut it into four identical (square) sections. Sand or plane the cut edges so that the individual sections can be glued together with precision later on.

14__Now turn the two matching sections (control the direction of the grain!) against each other so that the snowman's profile can be seen, then glue them together.

15__Glue the two glued pairs together again. The profile sides must lie facing inward, and once again a square blank is the result. By this point the snowman can be seen on all four planes.

Important: The cut edges need to be level in order to avoid gaps when gluing. Make sure that the profiles don't shift during gluing.

16__Clamp the glued blank between the chuck and the rotating pressure ring tip.

17__Use the 12-mm continental gouge to make an oval outer contour.

Important: Guide the tool with very little pressure.

18__Make sure that there is always sufficient material for the motif, or the wood might break. With some practice you'll be able to ascertain the thickness of the material by looking at the flying shadow. If you have any doubt, control the thickness while the machine is switched off.

19__The curve of the profile of the bottom side of the decorative sphere tends to be flat and is matched to the curve of the snowman.

20__At the opposite side the piece is rather oblong-oval (that is, more like a decorative egg than a decorative sphere . . .).

21__Turn down the curve on both sides while allowing a small stud to remain. If there isn't enough space remaining, use a skew for the last cuts.

22__Cut off both studs and finish the surface by hand.

Birch
Dia. 33 cm
H 15 cm

4 CROSS-GRAIN WOOD BOWL—OPEN

HELGA BECKER

Materials	
Tools	Gouge, 9 mm
	Gouge with Irish grind, 9 mm
	Parting tool, 3 mm
	Oval skew chisel, 25 mm
Wood	Birch, diameter ca. 35 cm
	Important: The blank must be cut as round as possible (with a power saw or hand saw) before working it on the lathe, to reduce the imbalance as much as possible.
Accessories	Faceplate, 15 cm
	Multi-jaw chuck (tower jaws)
	Acrylic paint

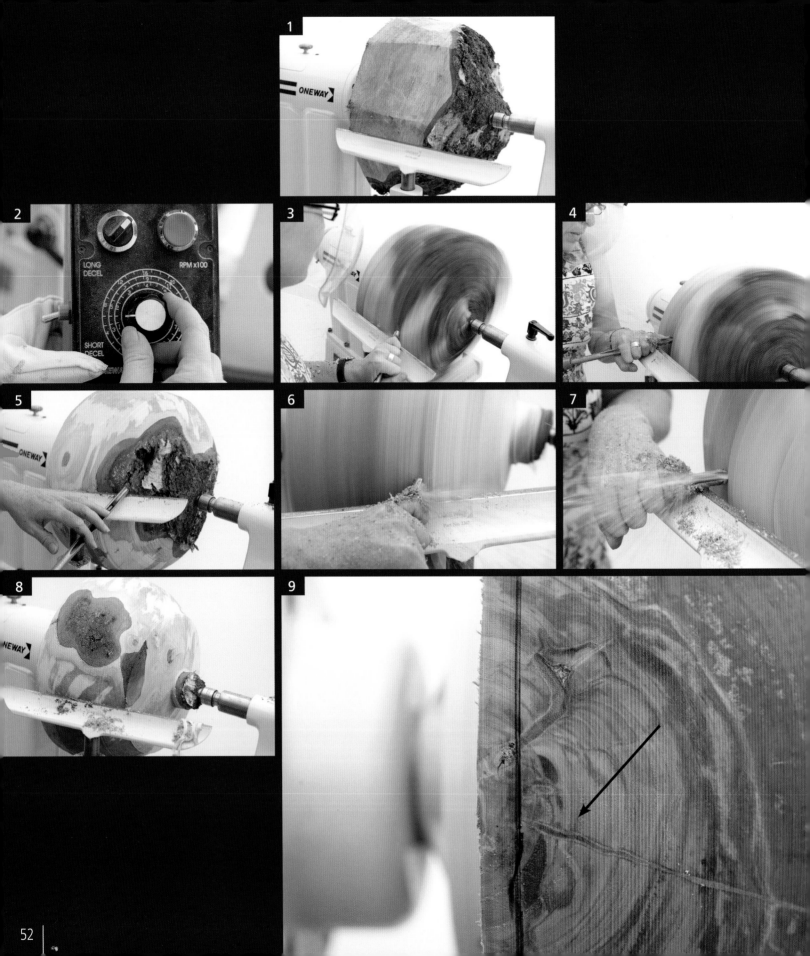

This bowl was commissioned by an interior designer. A modern white eat-in kitchen was to feature natural and colored wooden objects; I created a series of wet wood bowls of various sizes. Some of them were left entirely untreated. Some of them were painted with lively colors on the interior or exterior.

The important factor when working with moist wood is an even and thin wall, across the entire piece if possible. "Thin" is of course relative to the size of the piece. In the case of this bowl, it means about 4 mm. This allows for it to be practical and usable as a household item. For a bowl that's to be entirely decorative, the wall can certainly be thinner.

1__Affix the blank to the lathe with the faceplate and secure it with the tailstock at the right side.
Important: Blanks of this size should not be clamped to the threaded chuck—that may lead to injury.

2__**Important:** Check the set speed. It has to be matched to the size of the piece! An electronic speed control like the one shown allows for very fine adjustment of the rotation speed. It's better to be on the slow side rather than too fast. You may have to start out with the slowest setting.
Tip: If the machine still runs unevenly, you must work the blank by hand.

3__Plane the blank, that is, turn it round at the side. This kind of blank may have pieces of bark coming loose and breaking off, so I usually use a face shield for protection. The bubble-shaped shield allows enough space for eyeglasses, and there's enough distance between the mouth/nose and the Plexiglas to prevent fogging from your breath.

4__I use the Douglas or Irwin bit instead of the roughing gouge during this first step because the roughing gouge doesn't allow for good control of the exposed edges on the multi-angled blank.

5__The bark has now been removed and all of the cutting edges have been planed. Now you must remove the bark on the bottom side as well. There was some deep bark encrustation on this particular piece, so the curve had to be adequately adjusted.
Tip: With the machine turned off, check whether all of the bark areas, including the cambium, are completely removed.

6__Because the tailstock is still used for stabilization, the tool can't be guided from the bottom to the top. As we're still working in the rough, we can ignore the direction of the cut. The last shaping cuts have to be made from the bottom to the edge, for surface quality purposes.

7__The wet wood can be cut easily since it's still very soft. I always enjoy observing the flying bits of wood.
Important: The bezel must be placed onto the wood for an effective and clean cut.

8__A bast fiber (the bark area between the bark and the soft wood) can be observed on the blank. This bast must be removed entirely since it might dry out and fall off. The surface would then feature a straight plane.

9__Now we focus on the rim of the bowl. What you can see here is not a crack but the base of a branch that runs from the core (left) toward the outside. It shouldn't pose any problems when drying.
Important: The core can't remain in the bowl, since its wood presents the risk of ripping while drying.

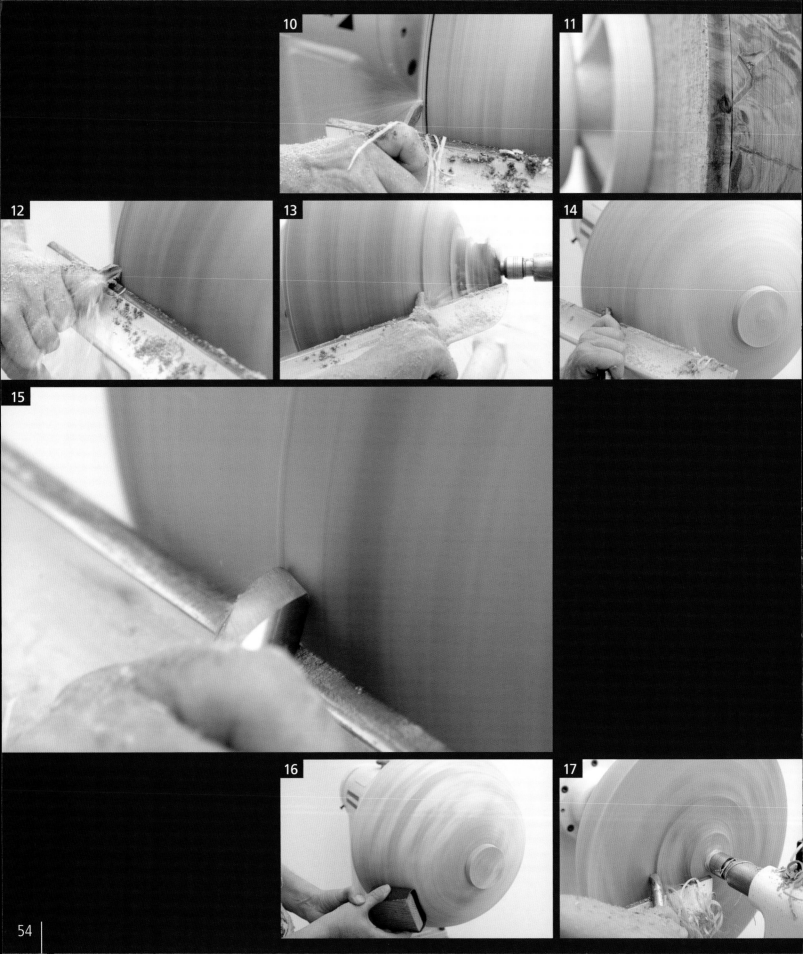

10__Use a pencil to mark the spot where the edge of the bowl will be, and to the left of this mark make a perforation with the parting tool, about 1 to 1.5 cm deep.

11__The core lies outside of the edge and the branch runs toward the edge.

12__Now work out the shape of the bowl. For now this is done by making cuts from the edge to the bottom, since there is still some material to be removed.

13__Make sure you have a nice curve without kinks or dents. For rechucking, a stud (footer) must be turned.

Tip: Make the footer as long as possible to achieve a large surface. When working with wet wood I use so-called tower jaws, that is, a multi-jaw chuck. Their grooved interior faces hold the piece over a large area.

14__To achieve a clean surface, make the last cuts from the bottom toward the edge, since only this method allows for cutting with the grain. The rotating tip must be removed for this process.

15__For these cuts the gouge with an Irish or set back grind works well. The blunt bezel lies on the surface and allows for the tool to glide smoothly.

16__After the contour is done, sand the bottom of the bowl. For such large and moist areas I only work with sanding linen and a sanding block. Round sanding discs aren't suitable because they clog up quickly.

Tip: When sanding moist wood, I start out with a grit that's one step below the one I would use for dry wood. In this case, I started with 120 grit instead of 180. Since the abrasive paper clogs up quickly with moist wood, it makes no sense to sand too finely. Usually 240 or 320 grit is good enough. If needed, the bowl can be sanded again after it's dry using special sanding accessories (e.g., the Kirjes sanding system with a flexible shaft and inflatable sanding rolls; see page 25).

17__After rechucking, remove the material up to the perforated edge. Since the rotating tip is still used for stabilization the work area of the tool is somewhat limited. The gouge with Irish grind is particularly suitable for these cuts, because the blunt bezel allows for a steep angle of the tool.

Important: Now the core at both sides of the blank must be removed.

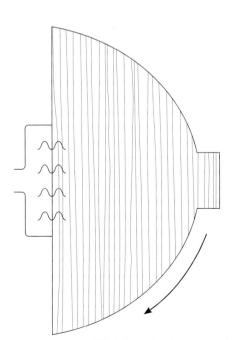

Work from the short toward the long grain

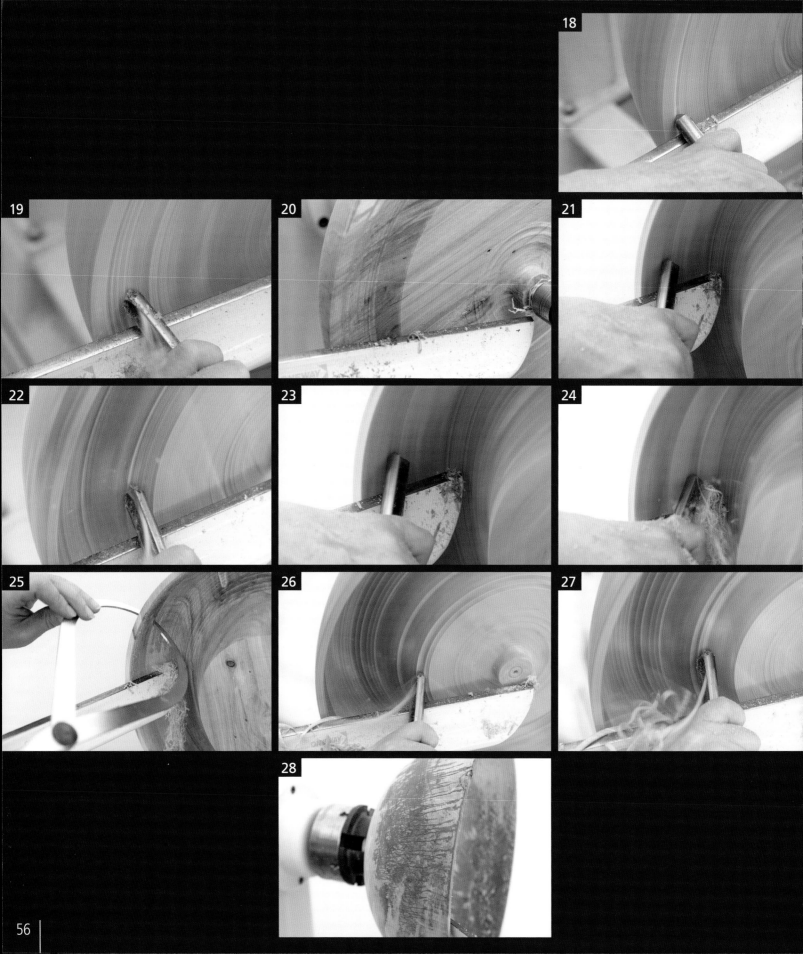

18__I prefer a conventional gouge for hollowing out because I prefer the lower angle. Generally, keep the following things in mind when hollowing out cross-grain wood:

Important: Do not start hollowing out a bowl from the center of the blank, particularly not when you are working with moist wood or when the diameter of the bowl is larger than 15 cm. The reason is that the piece will tend to bend and become oval due to the considerable centrifugal forces of large diameters. In the case of dry wood it won't be that much, but with moist wood it's considerable; you have to keep in mind the additional stretch and bend caused by the drying process.

If we hollow out larger objects from the center, the object is oval even before we reach the wall. Then it will be difficult to position the tool as it dances on the surface. Even if you succeed with the positioning the edge will be of uneven width. So the goal must be to leave as much mass as possible on the vessel in order to stabilize it. This is why we work in sections of 3 to 4 cm, from the outside toward the inside. In other words, the first cut is positioned at the edge and determines the width of the wall.

19__After the first cut at the edge, made from left to right, we provide some space with 5 to 6 cuts from the right to the left and with a width of 3 to 4 cm, and work the depth at the same time.

20__**Important:** Finish each cut before the edge of the tool touches the wood. This results in small steps remaining on the surface.

21__Then turn the wall of this first section to the final size with cuts from left to right. This results in the edge and the first section being finished before the piece can bend out of shape.

22__ 23__ 24__

Work into the depth and the center in several steps: cuts from right to left make room, cuts from left to right work out the thickness of the wall.

25__When using moist wood, it's very important that the wall is of even thickness across the entire piece. Check the wall thickness with calipers.

26__ 27__

When the first two or three sections have been finished and the cone of material at the center becomes unwieldy when you are handling the bowl gouge, you can remove it completely.

28__Due to the centrifugal forces and the heating of the tool, the sap of the wood is forced outward.

Tip: You should remove these streaks with abrasive paper as soon as possible, because the dried sap is difficult to remove.

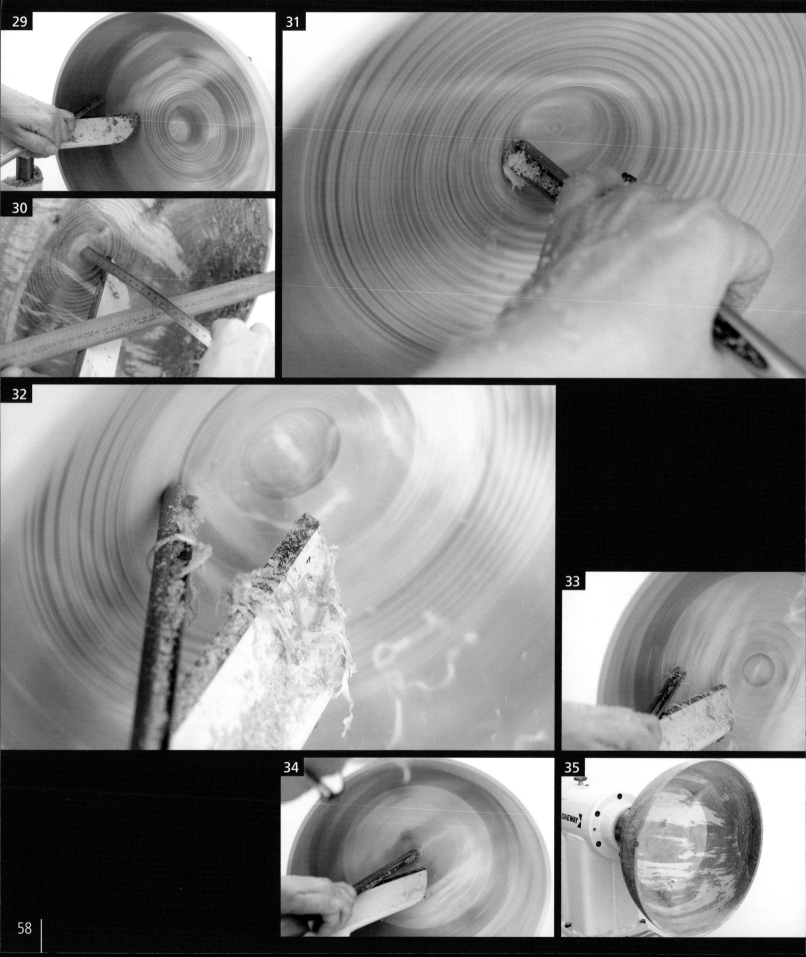

Drying the Piece

29__Once there is sufficient space inside of the bowl the tool rest can be shifted inward. This keeps the tool from fluttering due to the large overhang over the tool rest.

30__Continue using the same method, with cuts from right to left (to remove) and from left to right (to shape).

Important: Don't forget to measure the depth. Once you've carved out about three-fourths of the bowl you should know where the deepest part of the bowl will be located so you can create a nice transition from the wall to the bottom.

31__To do this, make pulling cuts (from the center to the left) on an area of 3 to 4 cm until the desired or required depth has been reached.

32__Cuts from left to right work out the curve. The positioning angle of the tool is very low (flat). Position it with the touching bezel somewhat to the left of the center and allow the cut to run toward the center.

33__The next cut is positioned farther to the outside (left) and also runs toward the center. Continue in the same way until you have completed the connection between the wall and the center.

34__In the best-case scenario, the last cut runs without interruption from the curve to the center and creates a harmonious curve.

35__Now you can sand the inside.

Important: Because the bowl has stretched and doesn't rotate roundly anymore, it is essential **to reduce the speed** when sanding. If the speed is too high the hand with the abrasive paper only reaches the protruding areas, that is, both of the narrow sides. Only when the speed is slow can the hand remain on the entire surface and reach the lower-lying planes at the long sides.

Now it's important to allow the bowl to dry as slowly and carefully as possible. I am not a friend of the shavings method—that is, I don't place the finished piece into a box filled with shavings and wood chips; my experience has shown that the surface tends to form a slight mold. Also, unwanted changes in color may result.

My drying technique is simple and proven to work with many pieces: I place the finished piece on my nightstand. The fact that the bedroom isn't heated plays only a minor role. The important point here is that this allows me to always keep an eye on the piece! At least twice a day (morning and evening) I can look at it without the effort of going down to the basement, the garage, or the workshop. I can react quickly in case the drying process doesn't proceed the way I want.

If the drying happens too quickly, I place the piece into a plastic bag for awhile. In the mornings and evenings I remove it for one to two hours. That allows the piece to breathe and to evaporate, which prevents the formation of mold. During the day the piece remains under its protective cover and I don't have to worry about it getting cracks while I'm away.

Another little tip: Turn the plastic bag inside out each time you recover the piece. This allows for the bag to dry out.

So far though, I've rarely used this plastic bag method. Most of my items have dried out well while sitting on my nightstand.

The only exception to my preferred method happens when I create large numbers of pieces for exhibits or fairs—there are limits to the space available in my bedroom.

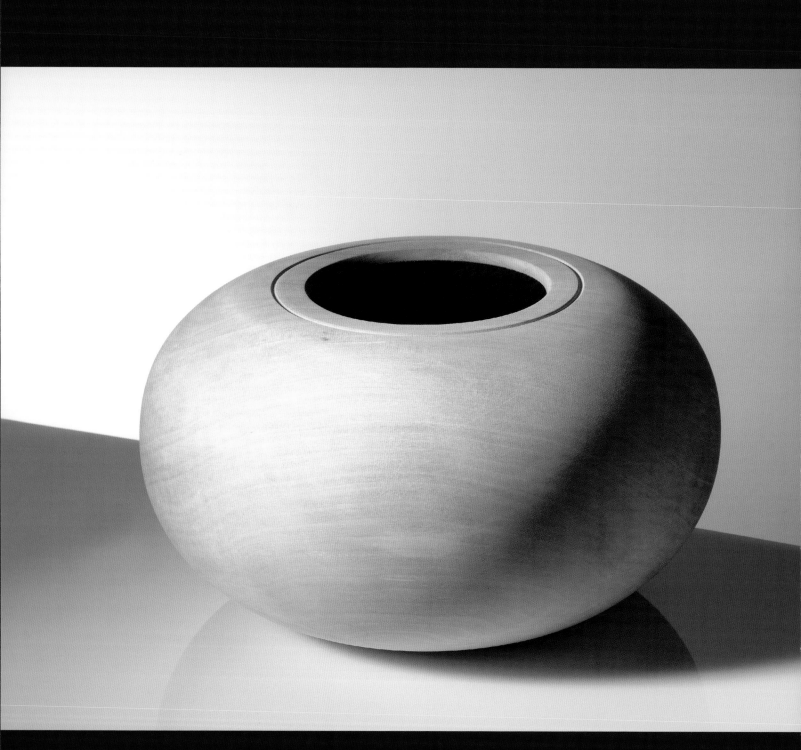

Birch
Dia. 26 cm
H 14.5 cm

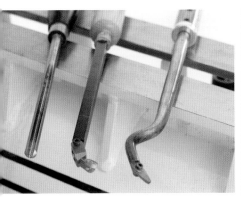  

5___CROSS-GRAIN WOOD BOWL—UNDERCUT

HELGA BECKER

Materials	
Tools	Bowl gouge, 9 mm
	BCT, 13 mm
	Giraffe neck with cutting tip (by Jo Winter)
Wood	Birch, diameter ca. 35 cm
	Important: The blank must be cut as round as possible (with a power saw or hand saw) before working it on the lathe, to reduce the imbalance as much as possible.
Accessories	Faceplate, 15 cm
	Multi-jaw chuck (tower jaws)

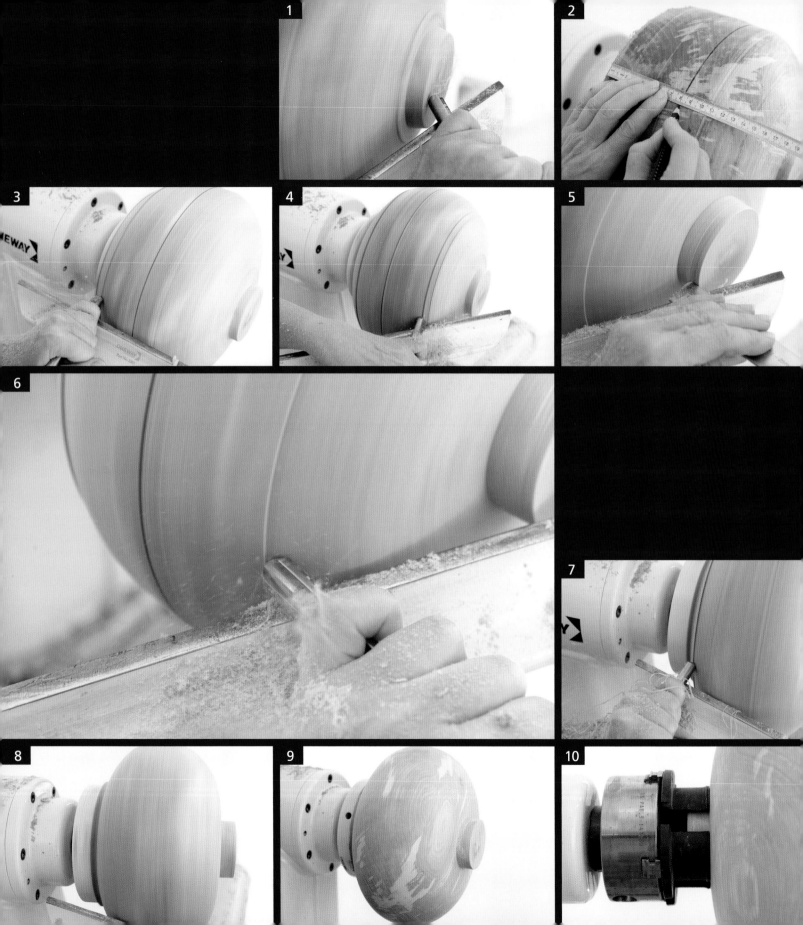

Using the second half of the blank from the previous project, I turned another bowl from wet wood. This vessel features only a small opening and was undercut quite a lot. This requires special tools that allow for hollowing out laterally and into the depth. With a hollow shape like this it is also very important that the wall thickness is even at all areas, so you should check the thickness as often as possible.

1__ Place the blank onto the faceplate and prepare it as in Project 4, *Cross-Grain Bowl—Open* (see page 52, photos 3 to 10).

   Important: Because the bowl should feature only a small opening, the screws must not be too far to the outside! They must lie inside the opening (see page 64, photo 17). Turn a stud, which can be clamped onto using the multi-jaw chuck (tower jaws), on the bottom side.

2__ The outer shape of the bowl should be given a symmetrical curve. The largest diameter (symmetry axis) lies between the bottom and the edge. First measure this center line and then mark it with a pencil.

3__ Using the bowl gouge, start removing material at the edges.

   Tip: Work in parallel toward the left . . .

4__ . . . and toward the right; this way you can check the symmetry.

5__ Finish the foot with the flat edge of a skew. It must match the shape of the clamps (cylindrical or conical). I use cylindrical clamps, so the foot must be cylindrical.

6__ After the outer shape is basically finished, rework the surface from the foot to the center line using the bowl gouge. This allows you to cut with the grain (surface quality).

   Important: Remember the bevel!

7__ On the left side of the center line you must work with very sharp tools, since the cuts from the center line to the future upper edge are actually made against the grain. Small, fine cuts and a very slow feed rate (so that every section is cut several times) may help.

8__ Check the profile of the shape often, and if necessary correct the curve.

9__ Sand the finished turned outer face (120 to 320 grit) and rechuck it.

10__ The multi-jaw chuck holds the stud over a large surface. The grooved interior sides of the jaws provide additional holding force.

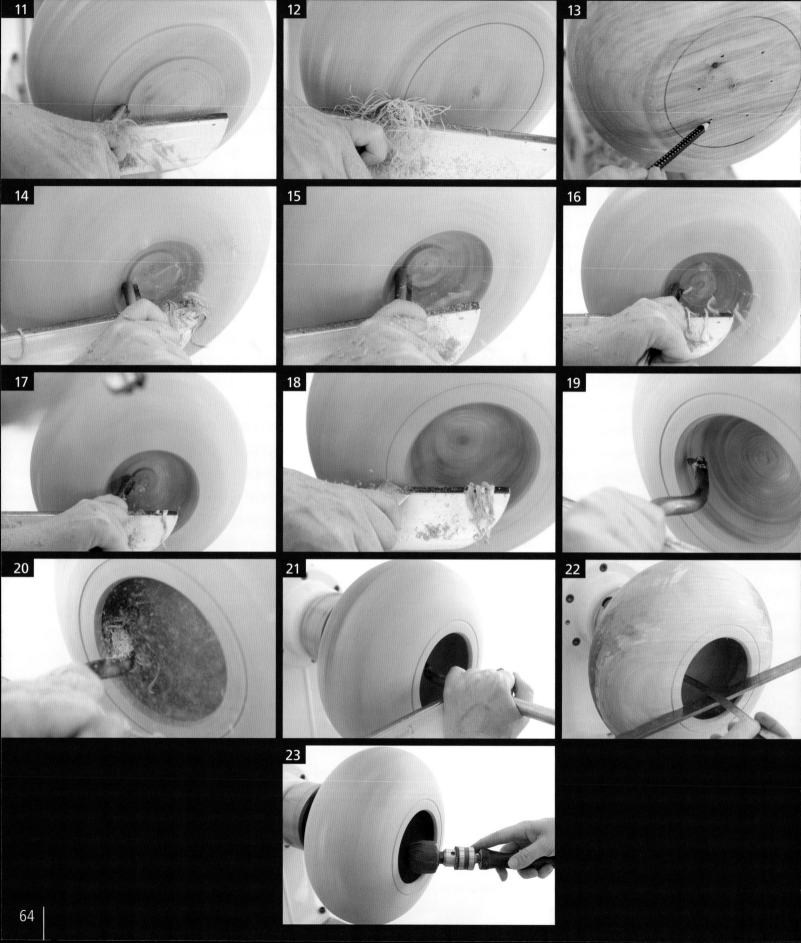

11__ Now turn the top side flat . . .

12__ . . . and pull the outer curve a little farther down. I've marked the end of the curve with a pencil. Inside this line the surface remains flat for the edge and the opening.

13__ **Important**: Observe the location of the screw holes. They must lie inside of the bowl's opening.

14__ 15__ 16__ 17__

Prepare the opening with the bowl gouge.

Tip: Try to reach fairly vertically into the inside with the bowl gouge (4 to 5 cm) and determine the diameter of the opening.

18__ To emphasize the opening a bit more, use the skew chisel to cut a small groove at a distance of 10 to 12 mm from the opening.

19__ The bowl gouge cannot be used for undercutting. A good tool for this purpose is the giraffe neck by Jo Winter, with a small cutting tip. Because of its curved shaft it even reaches areas that lie far to the inside . . .

20__ . . . and the HSS cutting tip effectively removes the material. It's sharpened across the entire crown so it cuts both to the left and the right.

21__ **Important:** The shaft of the tool must rest on the tool rest, behind its curve, or the tool might tilt toward the left. To get a clean surface inside the bowl you should make the last cuts from the center line (largest interior diameter) toward the edge (opening) and then from the center line toward the bottom. This way you will cut with the grain.

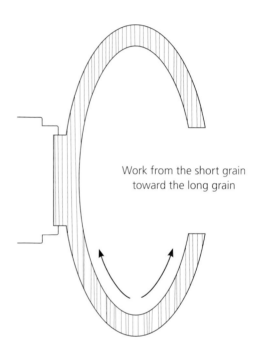

Work from the short grain toward the long grain

22__ To achieve an even wall thickness for the entire piece, you must measure the depth and check the wall.

23__ With undercut vessels, it is difficult and dangerous to sand by hand. I use sanding accessories like the Kirjes sanding system with inflatable sanding rollers. The spherical sanding attachment is perfectly suited because it can be formed to the curves.

Now the finished bowl must dry slowly. Check it, as often as possible, to quickly spot any changes. I dried my bowl on my nightstand, as described for Project 4 (see page 59).

Tulip poplar
Dia. 24 cm
H 24 cm

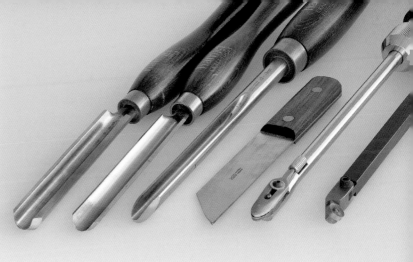

6___LAMPSHADE

HELGA BECKER

Materials	
Tools	Roughing gouge, 19 mm
	Continental gouge, 19 mm
	Bowl gouge with Irish grind, 9 mm
	Parting tool, 1.5 mm
	Exocet
	BCT, 13 mm
Wood	Tulip poplar, diameter ca. 33 cm, length 40 cm
	Important: The blank should have no knots, if possible. It should be of straight growth and must be cut perpendicular to be fitted to the faceplate.
Accessories	Faceplate, 15 cm
	Danish oil

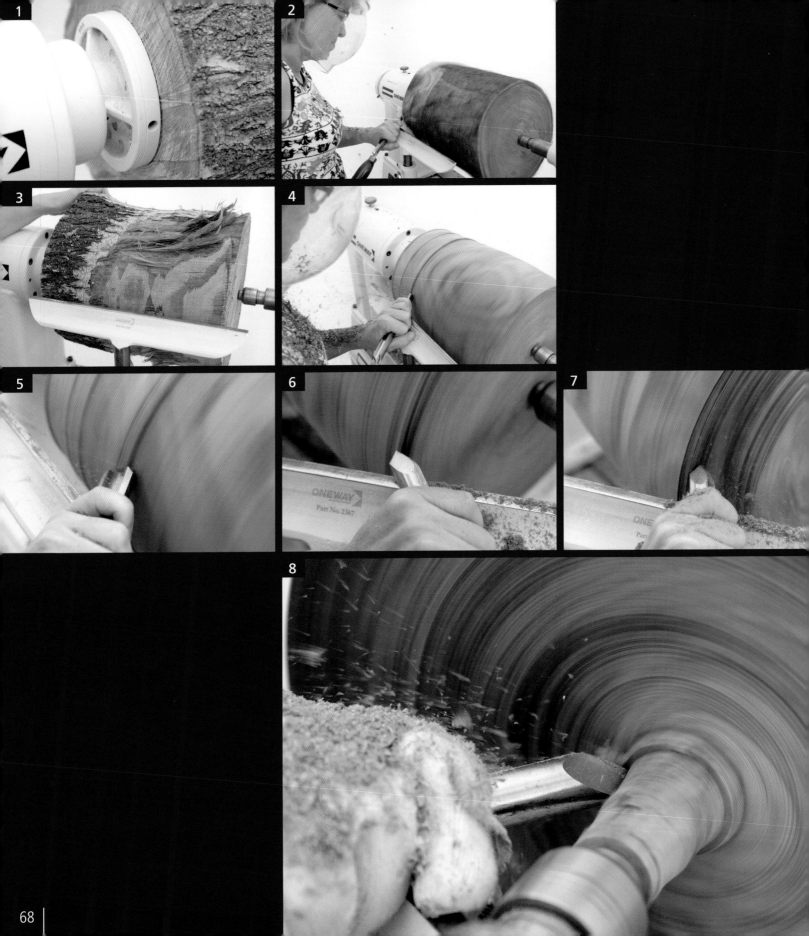

Earlier in my learning process, I used tulip poplar wood for a bowl project, and I'd wanted to create a very thin wall and check the thickness of the wall with light (see project 14, *Cowboy Hat,* page 163). However, as I learned, tulip poplar does not allow any light at all to pass through. Despite this fact, I chose it again for this lamp project, because of its extraordinarily beautiful grain and color and because this lamp was only meant to illuminate a small side table in our living room. It doesn't have to illuminate the room, but only shine downward. If you want more illumination, you should choose woods like cherry, maple, or apple.

1__Affix the trunk section to the spindle with the faceplate and with the tailstock stabilized on the right side.
2__For planing, I wear a face shield for protection against flying pieces of bark.
3__The coarsely structured bark features a thick inner bast layer with long fibers, which are rather difficult to cut.
   Tip: Make sure the bast layer is removed completely. Otherwise the fibers might dry on the piece and fall off. That would leave a straight plane on the surface.

4__Once all of the bark has been removed, the rough shape can be worked out.
5__The roughing gouge is the best tool here. It can be positioned nicely on the large surface of the blank and can remove a lot of material with each cut.
6__To turn the top side flat, I use the 9-mm gouge with an Irish (swept back) grind. Even though the rotating tip limits the available space for using this tool, it works very well here because it can be positioned at a steep angle due to its blunt bezel. The downward movement of the blade makes for a large and effective shaving.
7__While planing the piece, I discovered a knot that I didn't want on the surface. I decided to remove more material (about 2.5 mm) until the knot disappeared.
8__Except for a small stud for stabilization, cut the material back.

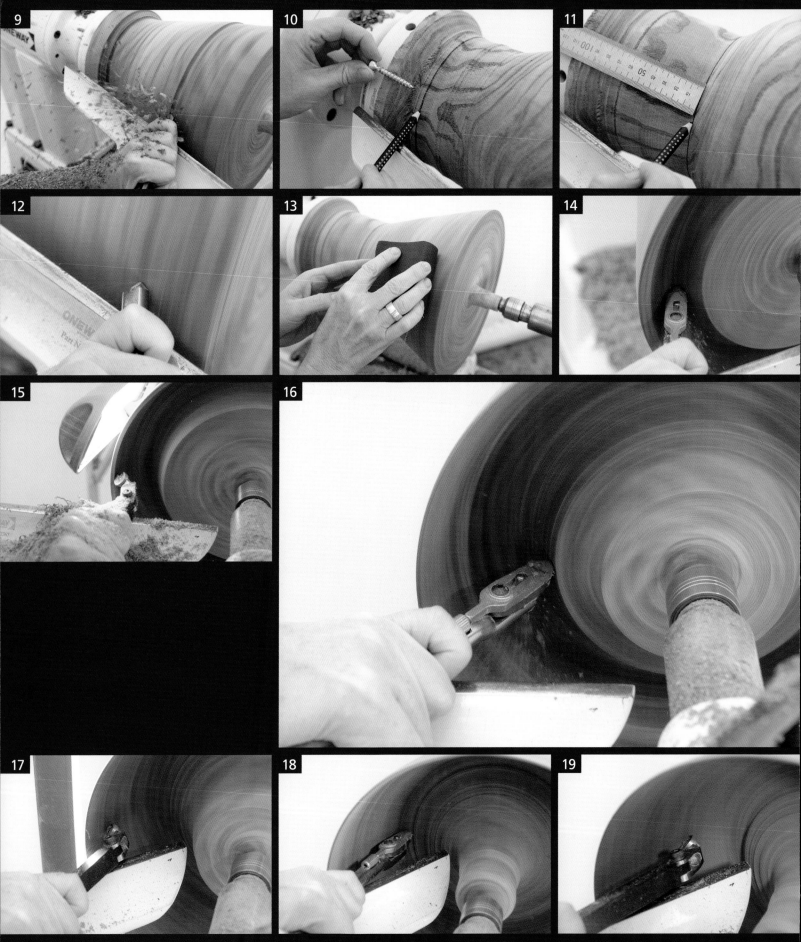

9__Now work out the final shape. The lampshade itself should be exactly conical, without bumps or dents, so it's important to repeatedly check the surface with a straight object (like a ruler, or a length of wood).
Tip: First form only two-thirds of the total shape, to stabilize the blank. If you start out making the entire shape, the wood might oscillate while turning, since the small diameter at the collar of the lampshade isn't stabilized enough.

10__**Important:** When determining the total length, keep in mind the screws that perforate the wood through the faceplate. Mark the ends of the screws on the wood. Make sure that the lampshade can be cut off in front of the screws later.

11__The lampshade should later be fitted with a small collar as a beautiful termination of the contour, and to fit the socket.

12__Make the last cuts using the gouges, starting with the large and going to the small diameter. This results in a good-quality surface.

13__Finally, sand the resulting plane with a sanding block. I used abrasive paper of 120 to 320 grit.

14__The blank can remain on the faceplate for hollowing out; it doesn't have to be rechucked. A very useful tool for both beginners and experts is the Exocet (which limits the thickness of the sliver—see the description of tools, page 19). To position it, the tool rest is held leaning slightly forward and cuts at the height of the axis. It works very effectively and it can remove of lot of material in little time without becoming stuck in the wood.

15__After clearing out with the Exocet, I use the BCT (see the description of tools, page 19) and reduce the wall to the right width, approximately 1.5 mm. It can be used with little pressure. The small cutting wheel is inclined at an angle of 45 degrees to the shaft.

16__Once the first section of the wall (about 4 to 5 cm) is done you can hollow it out again with the Exocet.
Important: When working with wet wood, you need to work swiftly. It's important that the woodturner advances faster than the wood is able to bend and stretch. Effective tools such as the Exocet and the BCT (or the hook, for experienced turners) are indispensable.

17__ 18__ 19__
Now alternate using the BCT and the Exocet. The tool rest must be set into the piece in order to best use the tools. The stud at the center of the piece can remain for as long as it's not in the way of the tool and its positioning.

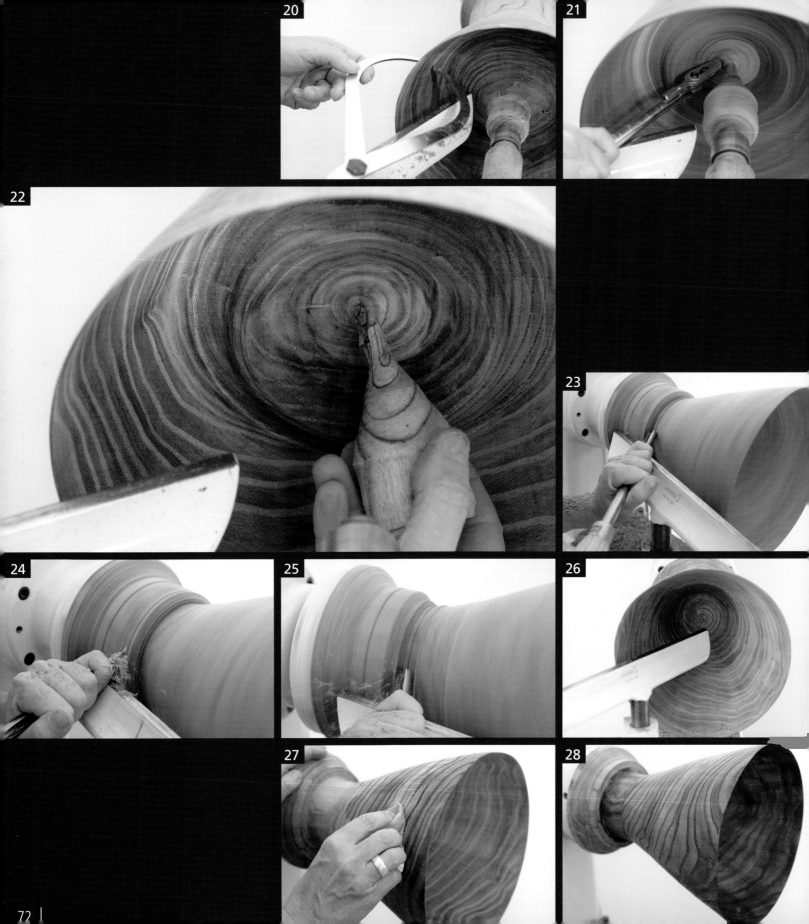

20__Because the wood doesn't allow any light to shine through the thickness of the wall, it has to be measured with calipers.

21__Finally, turn off the stud using the Exocet. It can be done both from the bottom to the stud as well as from the stud to the bottom.

22__The stud can be broken off by hand.

23__Once the interior is worked out as much as the exterior (two-thirds of the total length/depth), create the outer shape. The gouge is useful once again.

24__To do so, pull the cone toward the start of the collar and make sure you get a nice transition between the finished surface and the new one. Moist wood can cause small uneven areas at times, because the wood has changed its shape. Most of these variations can usually be sanded away (at slow speed!).

25__Now work the collar to its final size. Sand the newly created exterior surfaces.

26__Turn to the interior side again and work toward the depth. Proceed as shown in photos 17 to 20.
Important: Make sure that you create an exact cone at the interior. Keep in mind that the collar must be turned as a cylinder. It's important to measure the interior shape with calipers.

27__After sanding the interior completely (120 to 320 grit)—at slow rotation speed!—oil the lampshade on every surface. I use Danish oil, which emphasizes the color and the wood grain.

28__Use a clean paper towel or rag to polish the surface. The tulip poplar wood develops a warm brown tone. If you have help available to hold the lampshade, it can be cut off with a thin parting tool (1.5 mm). If you don't have help around, you should saw it off with a thin saw.

The socket for the lamp was fitted onto a metal ring with a diameter corresponding to the diameter of the lampshade at the transition between the cone and the collar. The lampshade simply lies on this metal ring, and doesn't have to be affixed to it. The cord is run through the collar toward the ceiling.

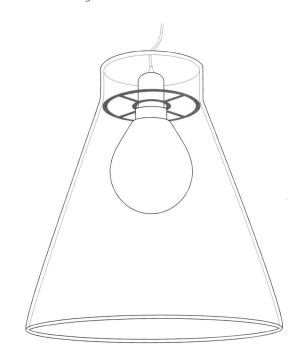

The metal ring is slightly larger than the diameter of the collar and therefore supports the lampshade.

Maple
Dia. 13.5 cm
H 22.5 cm

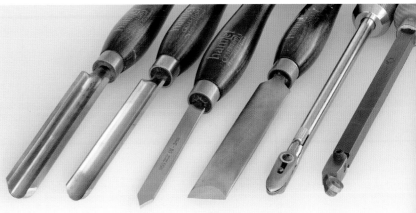

7___OPENWORK VASE

HELGA BECKER

Materials	
Tools	Roughing gouge, 19 mm
	Continental gouge, 19 mm
	Parting tool, 3 mm
	Oval skew chisel, 25 mm
	Exocet
	BCT, 13 mm
Wood	Maple, diameter 18 cm, length 35 cm
Accessories	Multi-jaw chuck (tower jaws)
	Packing tape
	Angle grinder with grinding disc or Arbortech grinder
	Steel brush for mounting to the drill or cordless screwdriver

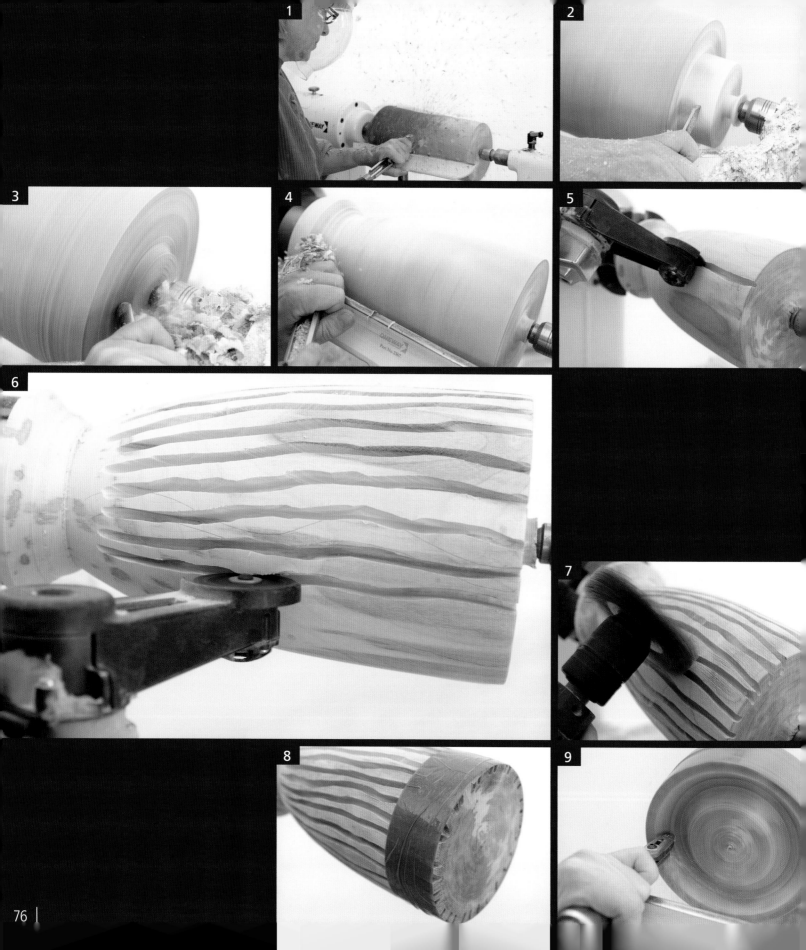

The maple trunk used for this project had been cut about six months earlier. Surprisingly, the trunk showed barely any cracks when this vase was created in July. However, a noticeable change of the wood's color had begun, featuring light and dark areas and fine green-gray embedded particles. I wanted to maintain this patterned look, which reminded me of moving aquatic plants, in the finished piece. So I designed the surface with structures, brushed surfaces, and openwork after turning it.

1__Chuck the trunk section between the centers and plane it.

Tip: Wear a face shield for protection against flying pieces of bark.

2__Turn a long stud for fitting the piece into the chuck. The length depends on the clamps you have at your disposal. I use the multi-jaw chuck, or tower jaws (see Project 5, *Cross-Grain Wood Bowl—Undercut,* on page 61).

3__After rechucking, turn the top side flat first.

4__Using the roughing gouge, you can work out the shape quickly. A continental gouge should be used for the last fine cuts to achieve a clean surface.

5__In contrast to the preceding lamp project (involving the turning of two-thirds of the outer shape, then hollowing it out, finishing the last outer third, and then hollowing out the rest), the exterior shape of the vase must be created entirely in one step before hollowing it out, because the surface will feature structures. This allows for a smooth structure in one setting without any patchwork.

Important: Even if the entire surface will later be reworked with structures and brushing, I always sand the surface beforehand, to assure that even the smallest areas that might be left untreated are totally clean.

6__Using the Arbortech grinder or an angle grinder with a grinding disc, cut slightly wavy notches into the surface. They have a depth of about 1.5 cm.

Tip: I make sure that the curve is slightly different with each cut, otherwise the structure will be too monotonous. Also, it's important that the notches at the upper edge are farther apart than those at the bottom, or the resulting structure will tend toward a spiral shape.

7__Once the entire surface has been structured, treat the elevated surfaces with a steel brush. A very fine second structure results, and the edges of the notches and grooves that might be slightly ripped by the grinder are smoothed.

Tip: To keep the surface from becoming discolored, use a brass brush on any woods (like oak) that contain tannic acids. Tannic acids react with metals like iron.

8__The rim of the vase should be so thin that it creates openwork sections and the narrow plant pieces become visible. To keep them from breaking off when hollowing out, tape the upper section with strong packing tape.

9__The Exocet allows for a quick removal of material, as described in Project 6, *Lampshade,* on page 71. Once again, start at the edge.

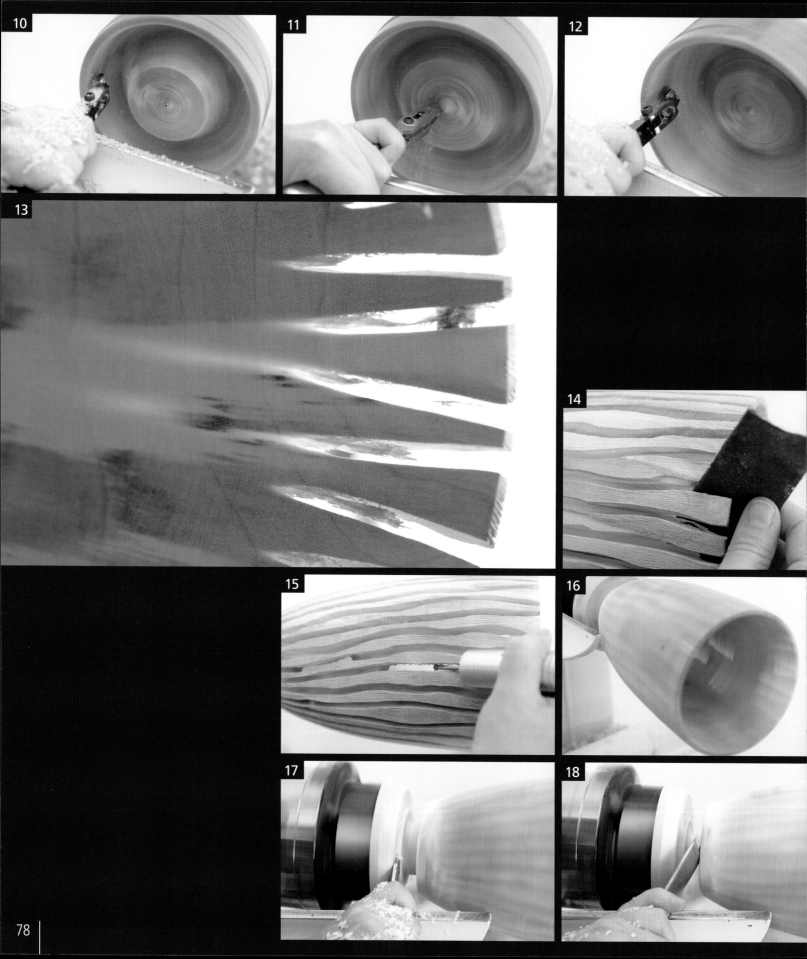

10__Hollow out a depth of 4 to 5 cm and work the wall with the BCT to the desired dimension (in this case about 3 mm).

11__Use the Exocet again for the cone in the center. It is also used for removing material into the depth . . .

12__ . . . and the BCT allow you to make the fine cuts at the wall. The photo clearly shows how the cutting wheel is positioned at a certain angle. It has already been mounted on the shaft with an angle of 45 degrees. But you can set the cutting wheel even a little steeper or tilt the shaft to the left while cutting (as I do on a regular basis). This makes for a less aggressive cut since only a small part of the blade touches the wood. This allows for very fine cuts—very important in the case of an extremely thin wall!

13__Now work into the depth, as described above and for Project 6, *Lampshade,* on page 71. After hollowing out, sand the interior face.

Important: Be very careful with the open edges of the rim! With backlighting you can see the notches as fine light strands on the interior side.

14__You can now remove the packing tape, and sand the notches by hand.

15__The entire surface will feature openwork motifs. Work them out with a small round cutter.

16__With the piece rotating, we see the openwork sections at the edge and on the surface.

17__Finally, cut off the vase on the left side except for a small stud. Use the parting tool first, to remove material and to make space.

Important: Before cutting off, it's best to measure the depth of the vase once again. The bottom should not be too thick (about 6 to 8 mm), as the wood is moist and the core has remained inside the bottom. If the bottom is too thick there's the danger that it will crack open around the core area.

18__To get a clean surface at the bottom (the parting tool leaves behind a rough surface) you should work with the skew chisel. In this case, the bottom has to be slightly undercut. Cut off the remaining stud by hand (with a Japanese saw).

Olive wood
Dia. 10 cm
H 15 cm

8____THREADED CANISTER

HELGA BECKER

Materials	
Tools	Thread chaser, 10 TPI
	Grooving tool
	Parting tool, 1.5 mm
	Roughing gouge, 19 mm
	Continental gouge, 12 mm / 19 mm
	Spindle gouge, 9 mm
	Oval skew chisel, 25 mm
	BCT
Wood	Olive wood, 10 x 10 x 22 cm

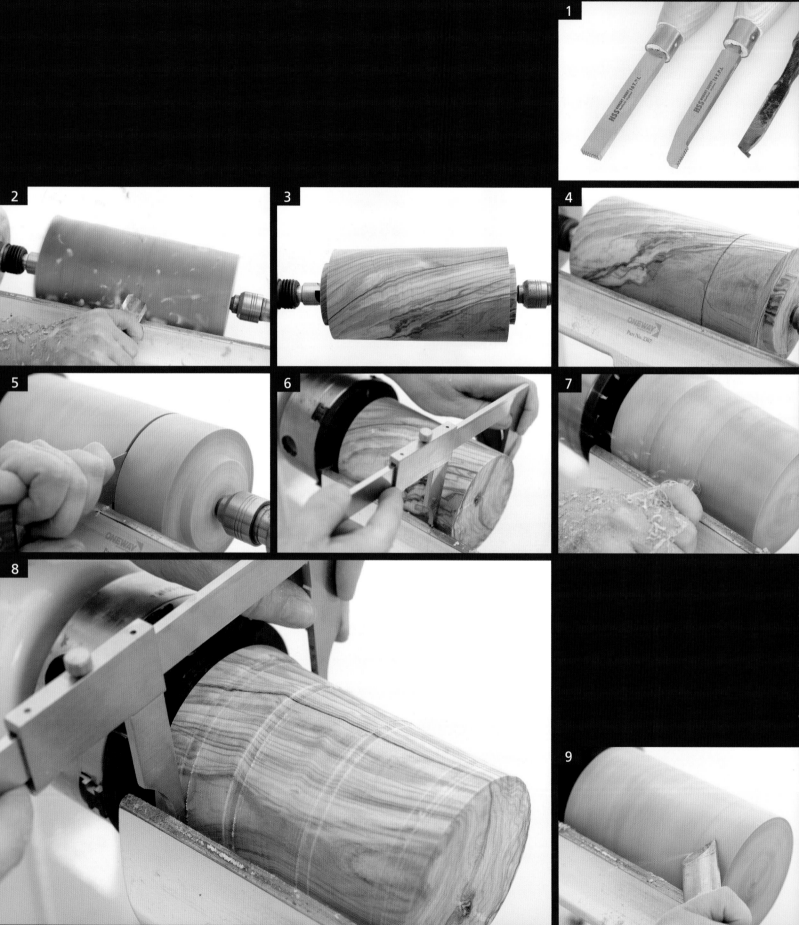

Canisters are fascinating woodturning projects. If they're also fitted with a well-made thread, there is an additional attractiveness for both the turner and the observer (or the client). So it's well worth learning this technique. I suggest, though, that you first try out guiding the two tools on a blank. It requires some practice and patience before the thread chaser can be guided to make a functioning thread.

Cutting Threads

Three things are required to successfully cut a thread into wood:

1__ ▪ *The appropriate tools: thread chasers (one pair) and grooving tool.*
We need two thread chasers of different shapes for the inner and outer thread. The thread chaser for the inner thread has teeth at the side, while the one for the outer thread has teeth at the front edge. These are always used as a pair. The type (size) of the teeth determines the thread pitch. A pair of thread chasers with 10 TPI (turns per inch) produces a thread with ten turns per inch, with 16 TPI the resulting thread is 16 turns per inch, and so on. A grooving tool (inside) and a parting tool (outside) prevent the thread chasers from running off the thread.
▪ *The right wood.*
Boxwood is a traditional wood used for cutting threads. But other exotic or local woods are suitable for this application if they consist of thin fibers and are dense, for example, hornbeam, pear, plum, lilac, yew and—as in our case—olive.
Important: The wood must be completely dry.
▪ *Slow rotation speed.*
The thread can only be cut at a slow speed of rotation. The best speed is between 250 to 300 rpm. Many modern lathes feature electronic speed con-trols that allow for setting the speed for thread cut-ting. But even if the lowest speed of your lathe is above 300 rpm you can cut a thread. This is how you have to proceed: at the slowest speed, you turn on the lathe and turn it off immediately. While the lathe runs out, make a cut with the thread chaser. It is a bit tedious and time-consuming but it works. I learned about this traditional alternative during my woodturning training in Switzerland.

Turning the Body of the Canister

2__ Plane the piece between the tips to its maximum di-ameter . . .

3__ . . . and provide both sides with a stud.

4__ Clamp the cylinder between the chuck and the tail-stock and divide the piece into the canister body and the canister lid, using a pencil. I always apply certain proportions: the golden ratio, or one-quarter to three-quarters, or (as in this case) one-third to two-thirds: one-third for the lid, two-thirds for the body.

5__ The 1.5-mm-wide parting tool divides both pieces without losing too much material.
Important: Don't try to cut the wood with one cut because the thin parting tool might become stuck. Instead, position the tool with two overlapping cuts. The notch will have a width of only 2 to 2.5 mm.

6__ So far the two blanks of the body and the lid still feature the same diameter. First determine the size of the lid . . .

7__ . . . and remove the corresponding material from the blank.

8__ The body of the canister should be cylindrical. If you cut back several areas along the length of the can-ister to the desired final size and then equalize the gaps to this size, you will achieve an even cylinder.

9__ Use the facing cut of the skew to remove minor un-even sections on the surface.

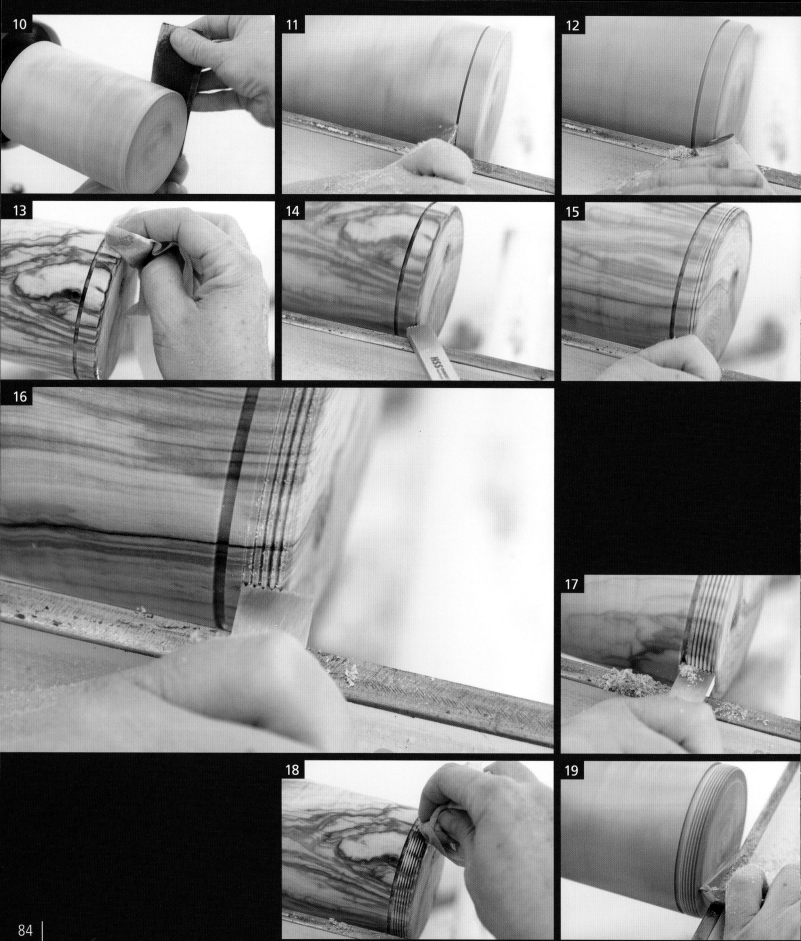

10__Sand the entire surface (in this case, with 180 to 400 grit).

11__In our project the thread is not "lowered" but it has the same diameter as the canister body. So when the lid is screwed onto the canister, it sticks out.

Important: Cut a small notch with the 1.5 mm parting tool to define the length of the thread and to prevent the thread chaser from touching the wood.

12__Give the front edge of the canister body a small bezel with the skew chisel so the thread chaser can be smoothly positioned and will not become stuck at this edge.

Important: The area for the thread must be absolutely cylindrical so that the inner and outer thread will run smoothly along each other later on.

13__Now oil the entire surface.

Important: Don't skimp with the oil, particularly on the thread surface, as the fibers should absorb a lot of it. They will be simultaneously plump and smooth, and thus easy to cut.

14__Set up the tool rest so that the thread chaser cuts at the height of the axis and parallel to the bezel. The rotation speed must be reduced to 250 to 300 rpm. Position the chaser with the second or third tooth (not with the first one!) and with slight pressure parallel to the bezel, shift it just barely to the left, take it off, and position it again at the beginning. Repeat this move once per second until you sense that the tool is gripping and is pulled forward by itself.

15__The first threads appear at the bezel. When you feel that the chaser is guided well inside the thread and develops its own forward momentum, you can gently increase the pressure and finally allow all of the teeth of the chaser to glide.

16__Now set the edge of the chaser's tooth parallel to the thread surface and allow the tool to progressively glide closer toward the small groove.

Tip: Oil the thread surface repeatedly.

17__Once the thread has been cut over the entire surface, every cut increases the depth of the threads. Apply slight pressure onto the wood with the tool.

Important: At no time should the tool stand on the thread. The result would be not a thread, but just grooves.

18__The threads are already clearly visible, and the crests are not torn but show rounded edges.

19__When the thread has been completed, cut it back to three or four thread pitches. This is enough to connect the canister and the lid later on.

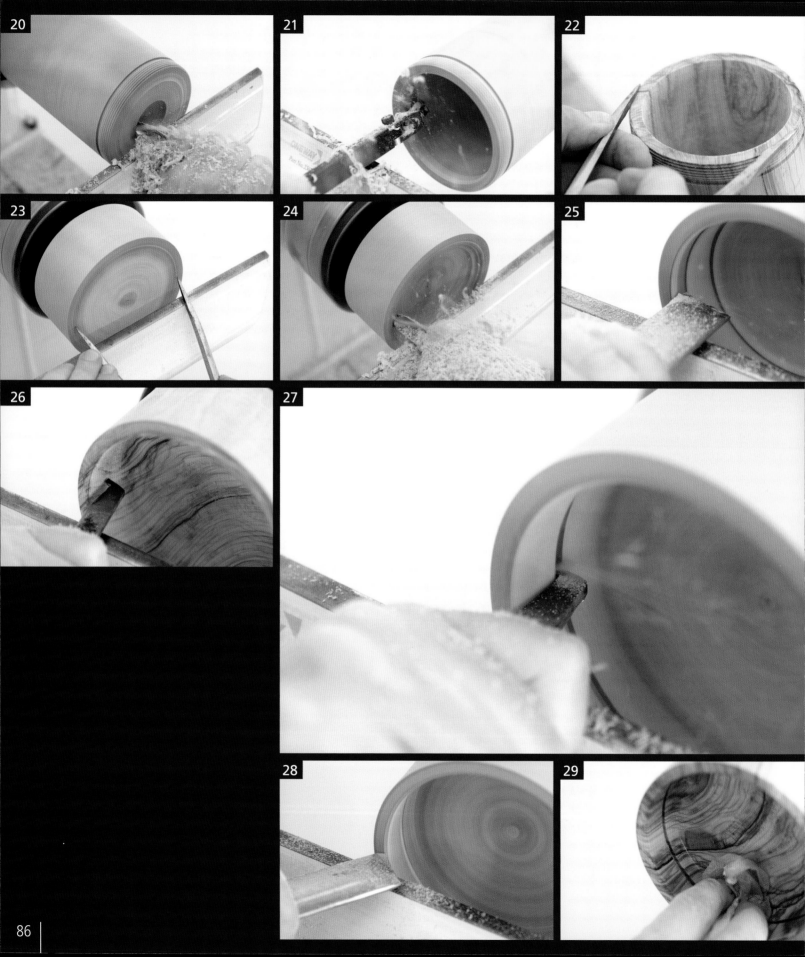

20__Hollow the canister out. The bowl gouge is great for cutting the dense olive wood. Set the tool at the center and positioned slightly to the left. While the tool is pulled outward it's set at a steeper angle. This way only a small area of the blade is cutting and the tool is not too aggressive.

21__Here as well, the BCT can be used at greater depths. Due to its square shaft it lies well on the tool rest even if there is a significant overhang. After the body of the canister has been completely hollowed out, sand and oil the interior.

Turning the Lid

22__For the inner thread of the lid, the dividers can measure the diameter of the outer thread . . .

23__ . . . and transfer it onto the lid. Now clamp the lid blank into the chuck.

Important: The diameter of the inner thread must be somewhat smaller than that of the outer thread so that the thread pitches will fit nicely later on (about 1.5 mm).

24__Hollow out the lid with the spindle gouge. You should approach the divider markings carefully so the diameter doesn't get too large.

25__Puncture the rebate itself with the skew. It works well to puncture the surface cleanly, cylindrically, and to the desired final size.

26__To make room for the chaser at the end of the thread, use a grooving tool to cut a groove behind the rebate.

27__This prevents the chaser from touching the wood behind the thread and stopping. You can make this tool from an old parting tool, a small scraper, or an old file, to your specifications and needs.

28__Once again, turn a bezel to the outer edge of the rebate with the skew.

29__Now oil the inner side—particularly the rebate—to prepare for the cutting of the thread.

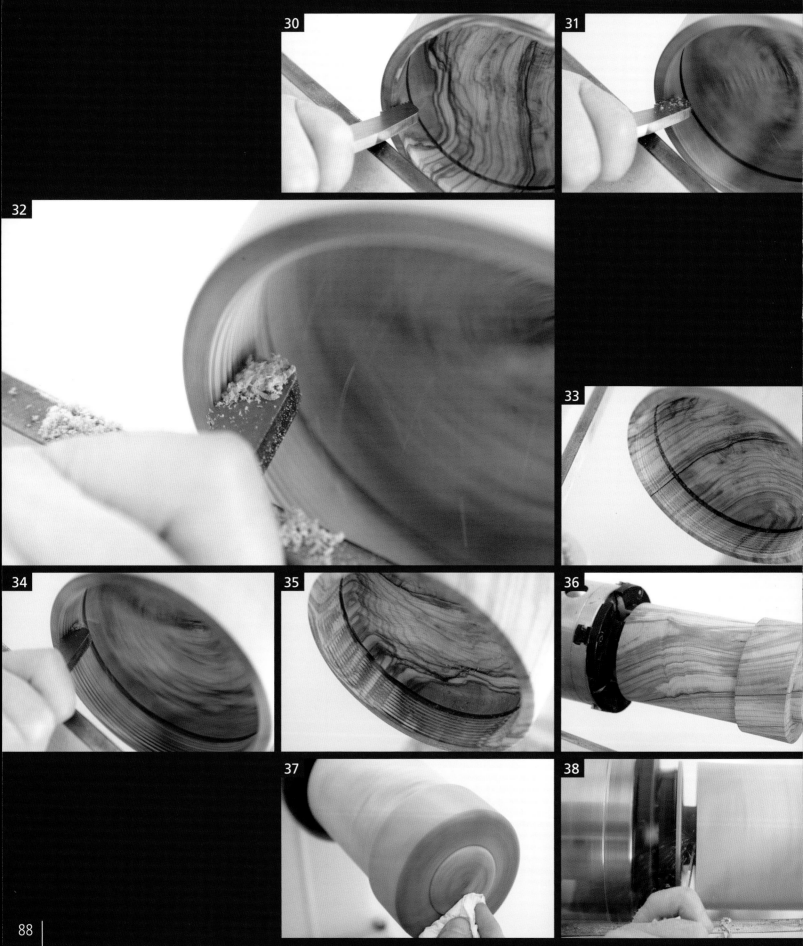

30__For cutting the inner thread, use the chaser with the teeth cut at the sides. The tool rest is set in front of the canister so that the chaser cuts at the exact height of the axis and is positioned parallel to the bezel.

31__Guide the tool, in this position, once every second over the wood (start with the second or third tooth) until the first thread grooves are visible and you feel that the tool is being guided (see page 85, photos 14 to 16).

32__Reposition the angle of the tool over several steps so that the toothed side of the chaser is increasingly positioned parallel to the rebate. This results in the thread pitches being lengthened into the rebate.

Tip: Continue oiling to keep the wood smooth.

33__Half of the thread is already visible. The pitches at the edge are already deeper, and toward the back they are still running out.

34__Now the chaser is running parallel to the rebate. Once the first tooth of the chaser reaches the rear edge of the groove, immediately lift off the chaser so that it won't touch the wall and destroy the thread. Now the thread is visible over the entire surface. The thread pitches are deepened by repeated steps and slightly more pressure.

35__The thread pitches are cut evenly to the same depth and the crests are not torn but nice and round. Once again, cut back the thread to three or four pitches. They start out right at the edge. Both threads have a nice grip. If the thread gets jammed when screwing it on, you might slightly enlarge the thread diameter, and the thread pitches could be recut.

Important: When sanding the lower edge of the lid, you need to be careful not to sand the start of the thread pitches!

36__To work the outer side of the lid, clamp the body of the canister into the chuck and screw the lid on. The continental gouge can be used to turn off the stud and to design the top side. You might want to use the rotating tip at first, just to make sure.

37__To remove the remaining material at the center, remove the tip. Now you can oil and polish the lid.

38__Finally, cut off the canister body on the left side. Due to the space and to waste as little as possible of the precious olive wood, I used the 1.5 mm parting tool. It leaves a more beautiful surface than a wide parting tool.

Tip: Before cutting off, measure the depth of the canister one more time!

Spruce
H 4.5 cm
L 27 cm

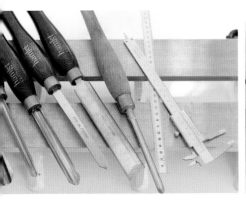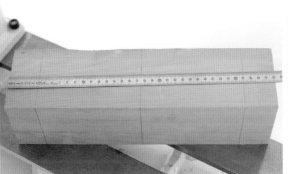

9 ___SPINDLE BOWL

HELGA BECKER

Materials	
Tools	Roughing gouge, 19 mm
	Continental gouge, 8 mm / 12 mm
	Parting tool, 3 mm
	Oval skew chisel, 25 mm
	Pointy tool
Wood	Spruce, 12 x 12 x 35 cm (cut square to precision)
Accessories	Small piece of hardwood for burning (in this case, ebony)
	Colored pencils
	Wax
	Abrasive paper

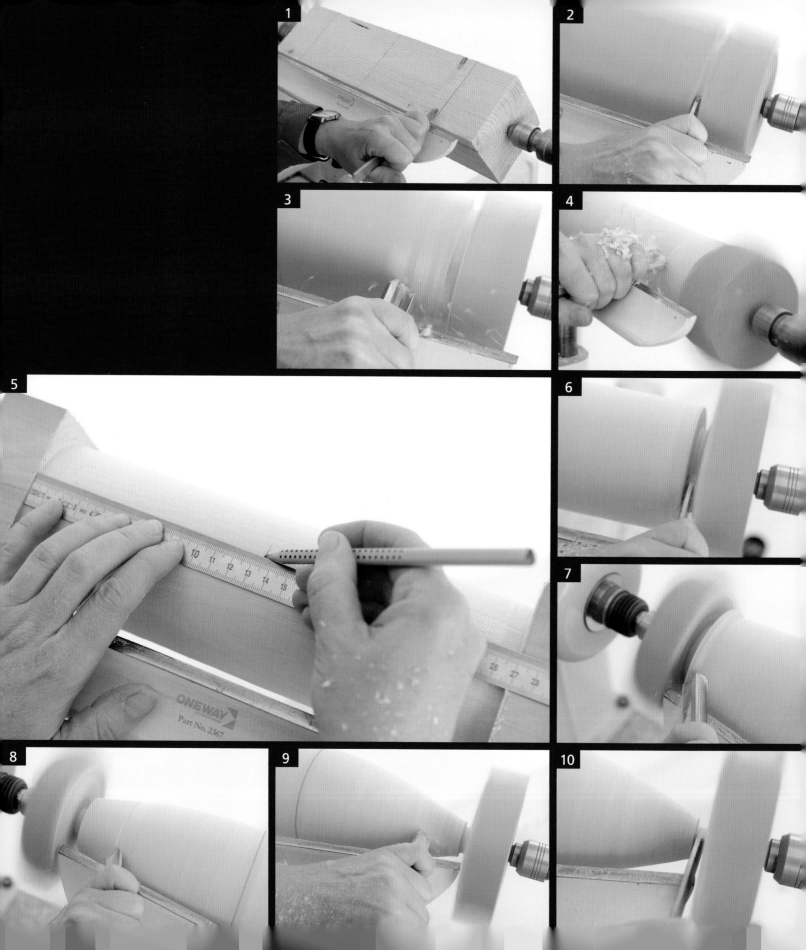

This project will give you ideas for making pieces that aren't immediately recognizable as being created on the lathe. We'll take advantage of the possibilities for further working pieces after turning, using sawing, cutting, and carving. This gives freeform elements to the creations. The method allows you to override rotational symmetry, which is often an advantage, but can also be a disadvantage and a limitation.

1__Clamp the piece between the centers. I've marked the beginning and the end of the spindle on the blank. Enough wood must remain to the left and right of the outer marks on the square piece (in this case, 4 cm). These planar sections are handy later on when sawing up the spindle (see page 97, photo 30).

2__Now puncture the ends of the spindle at the outer pencil marks with the parting tool.

Tip: Make two overlapping perforations next to each other. This allows for sufficient space for the tool and prevents it from becoming stuck. They also prevent the roughing gouge, which is used to work the area between the marks, from sliding outward.

3__Turn the middle section to the maximum diameter, while the angular outer sides remain intact.

4__Now mark the center of the spindle and work parallel toward both sides. This makes it easier to create symmetrical halves of the spindle.

5__Using the parting tool, cut off material at both ends of the spindle to make room for the shaping tool.

6__You can use the roughing gouge to start.

7__For finer cuts, the continental gouge (8 or 12 mm) is a better choice.

8__Control the symmetry on a regular basis and make sure that the curve doesn't become too thick.

9__With the parting tool, cut the ends of the wood except for a small stud. This allows sufficient space for the tool, and the contour can be pulled downward.

10__The stud will be about 14 to 15 mm thick. This way the ends of the spindle won't become too pointy.

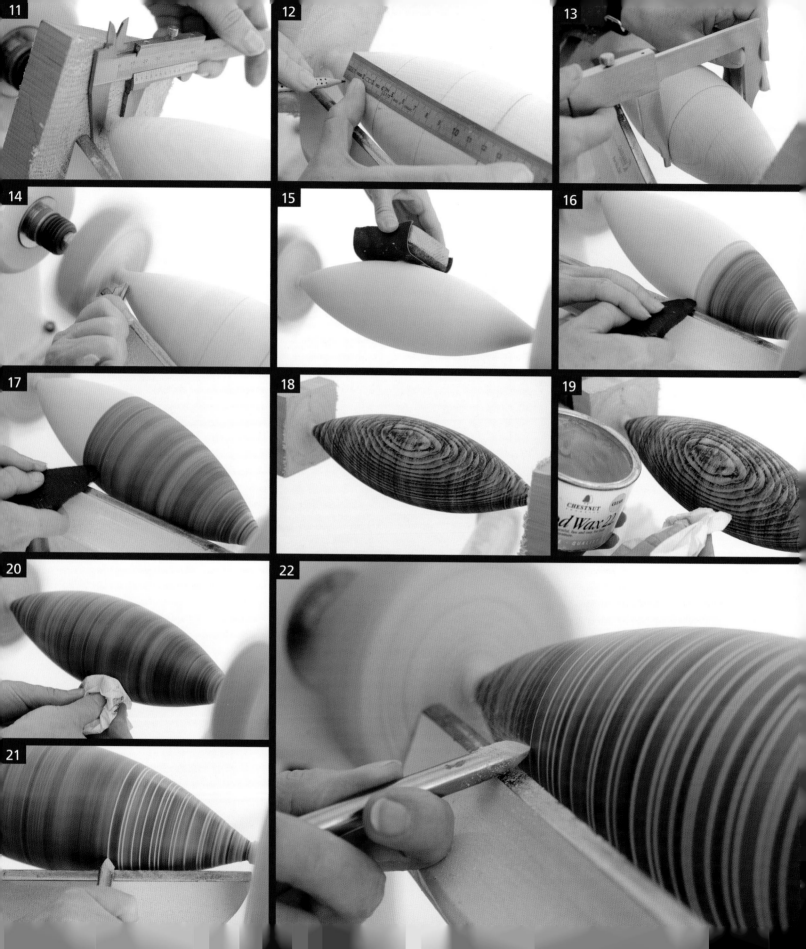

11__Starting from the center line I've marked both sides at a distance of about 4 cm.

12__This is where the measuring points are located, which I can use to control the symmetry of the spindle halves.

13__When measured at these points both sides must be equal. This makes it easy to create a beautiful and even curve.

14__Where necessary, correct the curve using the continental gouge.

15__Now you can work the surface with a sanding block and abrasive paper.

Tip: For very soft woods such as spruce, you shouldn't sand too much. The soft annual rings are easy to sand away and might leave behind open areas.

16__For a decorative finish, apply a dark base color.

Important: Choose a fairly high speed of rotation and press a hard "coloring wood" against the piece so enough frictional heat is created. I used a piece of ebony because I wanted a very dark coloration. Any other hardwood is suitable.

Tip: Try out different types of wood. You'll learn that each wood creates a particular coloration.

17__Don't bother trying to make the coloration even. It looks more natural when the burnt areas are slightly different. Don't burn the surface too much, either. The surface would have a thick film, which might break off.

18__The soft and hard annual rings can be colored with varied intensity. Their structure becomes more pronounced after burning and the grain is emphasized.

19__A layer of wax protects the burnt surface from abrasion and wear.

Tip: Apply the wax with the lathe off, so it can penetrate deeply into the pores. Make sure the entire surface is treated with wax without any extra wax remaining.

20__Wipe off the surplus wax with a clean piece of paper towel or a rag, and polish with the lathe running.

21__For the colored rings, cut grooves into the waxed surface. It looks more natural when the grooves are varying distances apart and not too far away from each other.

22__To cut the grooves I use a tool with a round profile sharpened at three sides. The pointy tool cuts very cleanly because of its three sharp edges. You can also use a skew. However, the grooves should not be too narrow for the coloration process coming up next. So the skew shouldn't be applied vertically, but rather, lying or hanging (the long tip cuts).

23__Based on my experience, the "ringlet technique" is best when you are using four colors. Depending on the combination you choose, your results can range from pastel-colored to bright and bold. Colored pencils have turned out to be the best choice in my work, and they are available in many colors and types. But you might also want to try out chalk, felt-tip pens, or other ideas.

Important: The colors must be light-fast.

With the lathe running, apply the first color (orange in this case) into the grooves at even intervals (about 2.5 to 3 cm). For each groove, resharpen the pencil.

Tip: Reduce the rotation speed, or the pencil will be worn down quite quickly.

24__Now apply a dark green color to the center, between the orange-colored lines.

25__Use red to color every second groove . . .

26__ . . . and finally, apply yellow to the remaining grooves. This results in all of the grooves being colored with none of the colors appearing in two adjacent grooves.

27__With the lathe off, apply wax once again to protect the colored grooves.

Important: Make sure that wax is applied to all the grooves. And always apply the wax "along with" the grooves, that is, going around the piece, not up and down on it. Otherwise you might smear colored wax from one groove to another.

28__Polish with the lathe running.

Tip: While polishing, hold the rag only briefly at any given spot and do not shift to the left or right. As you can see in the photo, the rag will at first take up colored wax heavily. Polish with new rags until no more color is visible on the rag. Now you can also polish with up-and-down motions.

29__The grooves are still filled with wax so they have to be cleaned out. To do this, while the lathe is turning I stretch the rag taut over my finger, and briefly press it into the groove using my fingernail. This removes the surplus wax from the groove while leaving enough wax behind to protect the color.

Important: Start each groove with a clean part of the rag! Also, leave the piece to rest overnight to allow the wax to harden.

30__To saw up the spindle, mark the center to the left and right of the two remaining pieces. Because of the planar side pieces the piece is easy to shift on the cutting table; it rests firmly and can't roll off.

Important: The sawing step requires total concentration and care!

31__After sawing up the piece, saw the side sections off from the spindle halves (by hand if necessary) and round the points with a file and sanding linen. The interior of the two spindle halves can be hollowed out with carving or cutting tools. I used an Arbortech grinder with a 50-mm cutting wheel.

Important: Clamp the spindle firmly when cutting so you can use both hands, and don't run the risk of injuring your hand by holding the piece with the cutter or grinder.

Maple
Dia. 9.5 cm
H 5.5 cm

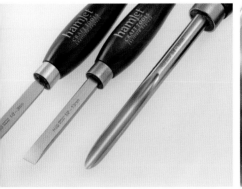  

10___JERUSALEM BOWL

ELI AVISERA

Materials	
Tools	Avisera tools
	Bowl gouge, 9 mm
	Flat chisel, 12 mm
	Parting tool, 3 mm
	Spindle gouge, 8 mm (optional)
Wood	Maple (as light as possible!), diameter 100 mm, height 60 mm
Accessories	Spigot chuck
	Bleaching agent

Because Eli travels a lot, he came up with the idea of making small copies of his pieces, to allow him to take as many of his designs with him as possible. He wanted to show them to potential buyers as samples, and take orders. Meanwhile, however, these small and delicate pieces themselves have become popular with galleries and collectors. Their technical execution is just as fine as that of the large pieces, and they take up less space in the customers' homes. You might want to re-create the projects in small format, or transfer the techniques to large pieces.

The Jerusalem bowl is named for the special design on the outer side, which is based on the profile of the stones that are traditionally used in Jerusalem for building.

At the start of this project, Eli decided he had to create an important tool first. This was so surprising and funny (he is always good for a joke) that I want to share that process with you:

1 to 10__

Eli clamped a pencil into the long pliers of the One-way talon chuck, and in no time, with a narrow skew, fabricated a useful tool.

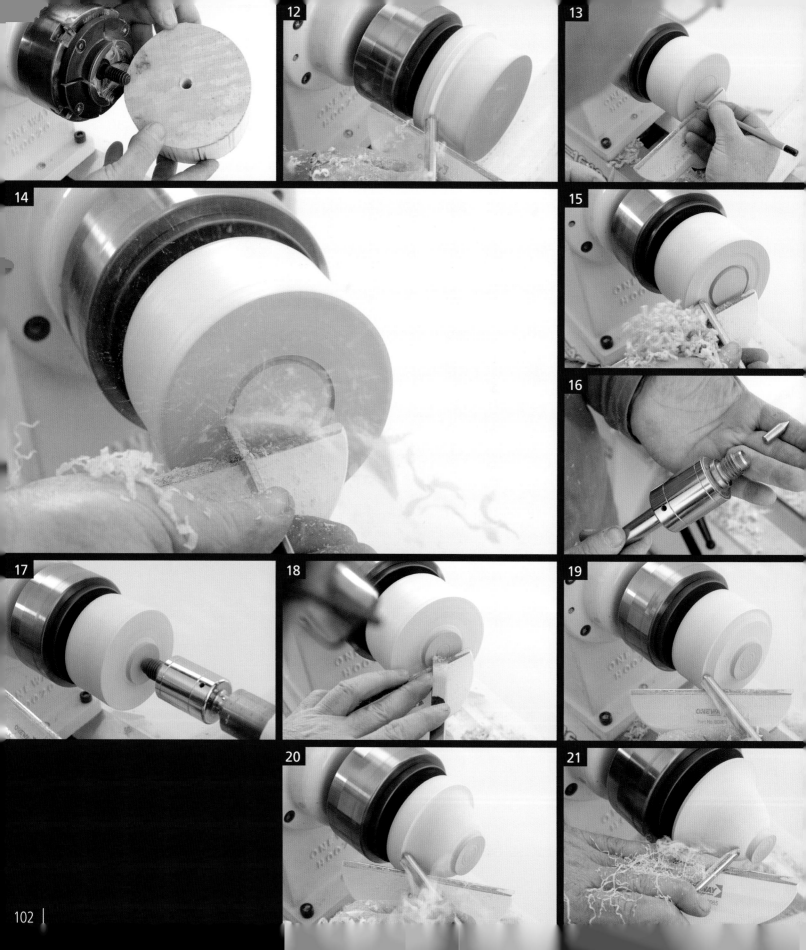

11__Drill the blank and clamp it to the chuck with the screw.

12__Using the bowl gouge, turn the diameter to the desired size, providing for a smooth rotation.

13__Now turn the bottom flat with the bowl gouge, and mark the diameter of the foot.

14__Using the parting tool, perforate the foot to the desired depth.

15__The extra material at the bottom of the bowl can be removed to the depth of the foot with the bowl gouge. The bottom should be slightly undercut.

16__For the blank to be precisely aligned when re-chucking later, Eli uses a little trick. The centering tip is removed from the pressure ring.

17__The tip of the pressure ring inside the tail spindle is then pressed forcefully against the blank, so that the ring marks the bottom of the bowl. This ring allows for aligning the piece again later on.

18__To avoid needing to remove the imprint of the ring later, it's hidden with one or several additional grooves and becomes part of the decoration.

19__Use the bowl gouge to continue shaping the outer form.

20__Work out a bell shape with the abutting bezel and long cuts. The diameter of the foot is reduced to 25 to 30 mm.

21__At the blind spot between the foot and the curve, Eli uses a small spindle gouge. Despite the pulling cut, it produces a clean surface.

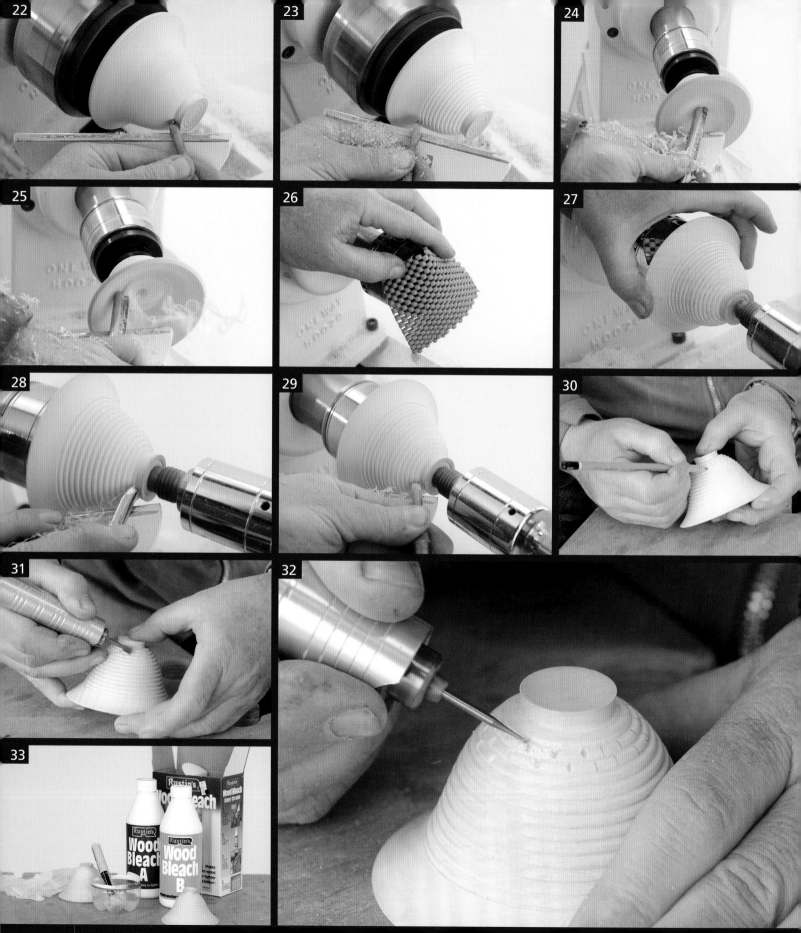

22__For the fine profile he uses a carbide drill bit at an angle of 45 degrees and adds a small groove. To stabilize it, the drill bit was filled with epoxy resin. This reduces vibrations that can occur through the thinner parts of the bit.

23__Cut a shallower groove with slight movements of the drill to the right and left. Experienced woodturners can produce this profile with a small spindle gouge. Mark it first. Then sand the surface, through 400 grit.

24__Now clamp the blank. Here we used a small specialized mini-chuck.

25__Work the material out, and smooth the surface.
Important: Keep in mind that the grooves in the surface have been worked from the outside. Don't work your sides down too thin!

26__Now work down the foot. Place a piece of anti-slip material on the jaws of the chuck, against the bowl.

27__Align the bowl using the pressure ring (without the tip!).

28__Work the cylinder of the base.

29__If necessary, adjust the groove again with a drill bit (or the small spindle gouge).

30__Next, draw lines for vertical notches on the grooved surface, marking the individual "stones." Stagger the notches from groove to groove.

31__Create small notches on the pencil marks with a bowl gouge.

32__Finally, work the surface of each individual "stone" to mimic a carved surface.

33__When the piece is completed, bleach it. Use a bleaching product made for the type of wood you are using.
Important: Bleaching chemicals can be hazardous. Be sure to follow the manufacturer's instructions.

Maple
W 8 cm
L 8 cm

11___SQUARE BOWL

ELI AVISERA

Materials	
Tools	Avisera tools
	Skew, 19 mm
	Small spindle gouge, 8 mm
	Bowl gouge, 9 mm
Wood	Maple (as light as possible), 80 x 80 x 20 mm, planed
Accessories	Sponge brush
	Stain

This attractive small bowl features a contrast between black and white, as well as the contrast between the basic square shape and the soft curves of the hollows. This project can be re-created at larger dimensions. However, you should use a threaded chuck or a screw inside the chuck when starting out, particularly if the blank is deep enough.

1__First, center the blank precisely with two diagonal pencil marks, so that the square basic form is maintained. Then, place it onto the jaws of the chuck and align it with the tailstock. Remove the centering tip from the pressure ring and press the blank against the jaws with the ring only. This way the centering ring leaves a mark, which will make rechucking easier later on.

2__Now scribe the diameter of the foot. This diameter depends on the size of the bowl (you want beautiful proportions!), and on the clamping options of the chuck, that is, the size of the jaws. Eli uses the Oneway talon chuck, which allows for a minimum diameter of 45 mm.

3__Using the small Avisera spindle gouge, first remove as much material at the edges as is required for the height of the foot, applying only little pressure. The sides of the gouge are abraded and allow for a clean cut, while the tool is well-positioned on the edges.

4__Each cut works out the foot more clearly. Position the tool to the far left, to offer a larger area of the blade.

5__Here you can clearly see the twin bezel, which Eli used to grind his tools. The blade becomes sharp and cuts the surface perfectly.

6__Now rechuck the blank and clamp the foot into the chuck. Make sure that the edges are aligned precisely on the same level.

7__The bowl gouge is carefully positioned at the edges (slight pressure!) and guided inward. Only a little material is removed at the edges. They are slightly turned over. Work toward the desired depth at the inside. The tool is turned up to the right and the bezel abuts.

8__When the interior face is finished, with the lathe turned off sand it with a sanding pad.

9__Make sure you sand with the grain. Use 180, 240, and 320 grits consecutively.

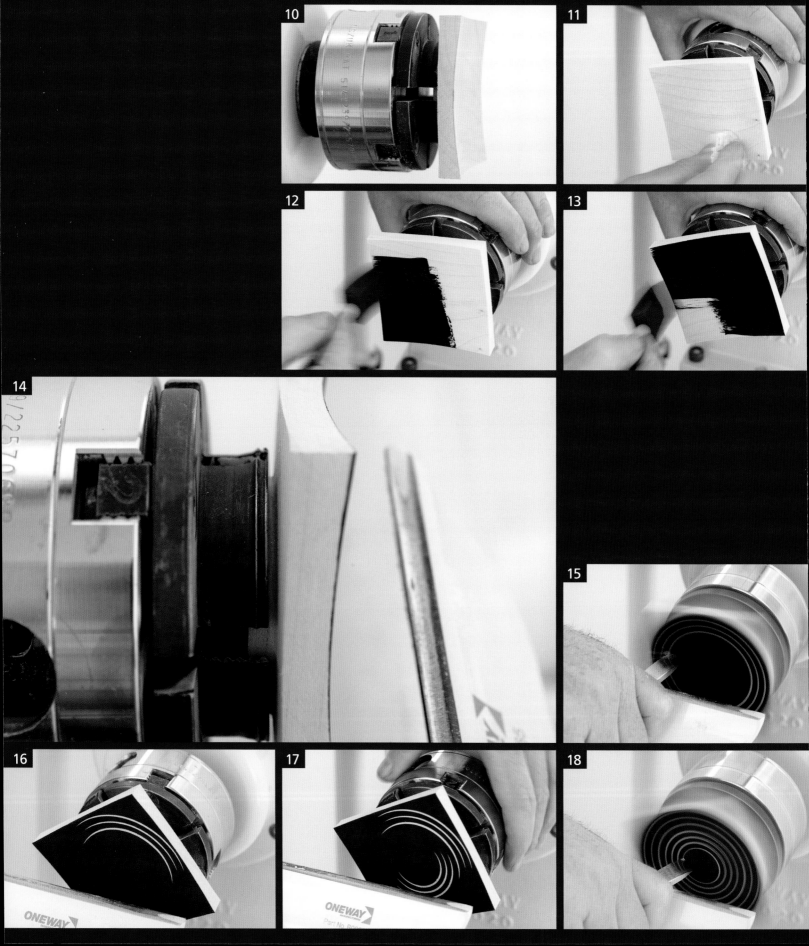

10__Also sand the outer edges without rounding them. The photo shows how thick the material is so far.

11__Moisten the surface with a rag or a small sponge, so the remaining loose fibers will stand up. Once the surface is dry again, these fibers are sanded with a final sanding using 400 grit. Don't use too much water!

Important: Moistening is important here because otherwise the fibers would stand up during the later bleaching treatment. At that point, though, they wouldn't be able to be sanded away.

12__Using a foam brush, apply the stain swiftly, following the direction of the grain. Because the stain absorbs rather well, you should only take up a little at a time with your brush.

13__Work wet-on-wet in order to evenly apply the color. The stain dries very quickly. You can speed up the drying process by rotating the piece on the lathe or by applying a hot-air gun.

Important: Keep enough distance between the hot-air gun and the piece, so the stain doesn't bubble.

14__To create the pattern on the inside of the bowl, loosen the chuck somewhat once the stain is completely dry, and tip the edge of the blank slightly forward. Clamp the chuck again in this position.

15__Using the long tip of the narrow skew chisel, cut the fine grooves into the surface. The skew cuts the grooves so cleanly that they don't have to be sanded again.

16__The grooves can only be noticed on the area that's tipped toward the front.

17__To shift the grooves, the next edge is presented, that is, taken forward in the chuck.

18__On the rotating piece, the grooves can be seen as adjacent circular rings.

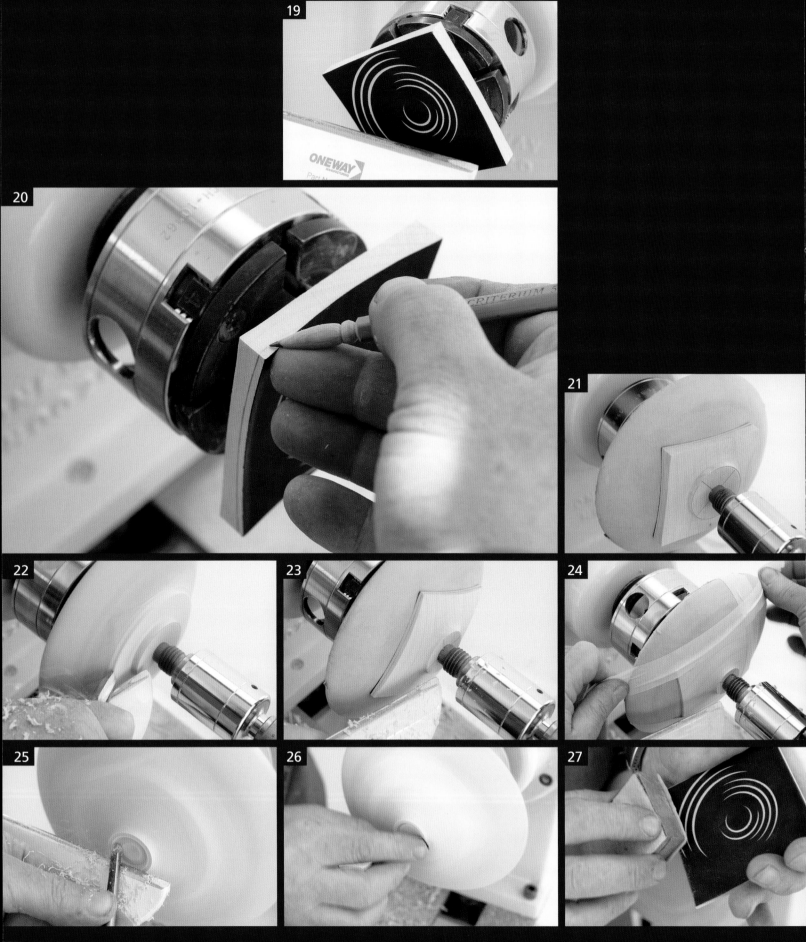

19__For the two interior grooves the lateral face was tilted forward, not the third corner of the piece.

20__Now the bottom side of the bowl must be finished while turning the face of the bowl very thinly. Mark the intended wall thickness with a pencil at the edges.

21__To keep the edges from breaking off, and from getting any clamp marks, fit the blank to an auxiliary chuck. For this purpose, Eli has glued neoprene onto a shallowly curved disc of plywood (foam rubber also works well) and clamped it into the chuck. The piece is aligned at the bottom side of the foot using the centering ring and pushed against the auxiliary chuck (slight pressure).

22__Now shape the bottom side with the spindle gouge.

23__Keep controlling the wall thickness.

24__Turn the foot down to a diameter of about 23 mm. To allow the bottom side of the foot to be worked, tape the bowl onto the auxiliary chuck at all four sides. The rotating tip can now be removed.

25__Using the small spindle gouge, turn the foot until the centering ring has disappeared. Give the junction from the foot to the bottom of the bowl a harmonious curve.

26__Sand the foot and the open face of the bottom side with the lathe rotating. Then remove the packing tape and press the bowl by hand against the auxiliary chuck with the lathe off. This results in the edges being supported with the sanding pad while you sand by hand. Now moisten the bottom face and sand it again. Protect the surface with wax or spray paint.

27__Finally, lightly sand the edges with 400-grit paper, so that the black surface is bordered by a thin, light-colored line.

Important: Make sure you don't sand into the finished surface!

Boxwood
Dia. 6.5 cm

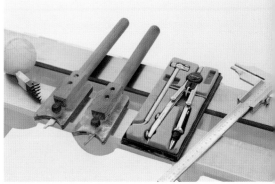

12____CHINESE SPHERE

CHRISTIAN DELHON

Materials	
Tools	Special tool kit for Chinese spheres with support
	Basic tool kit
	Spindle gouge
Wood	Boxwood
Accessories	Spherical chuck made of plywood by Christian Delhon
	Hand and tool base with horizontal table
	Calipers
	Dividers
	Abrasive pad or paper

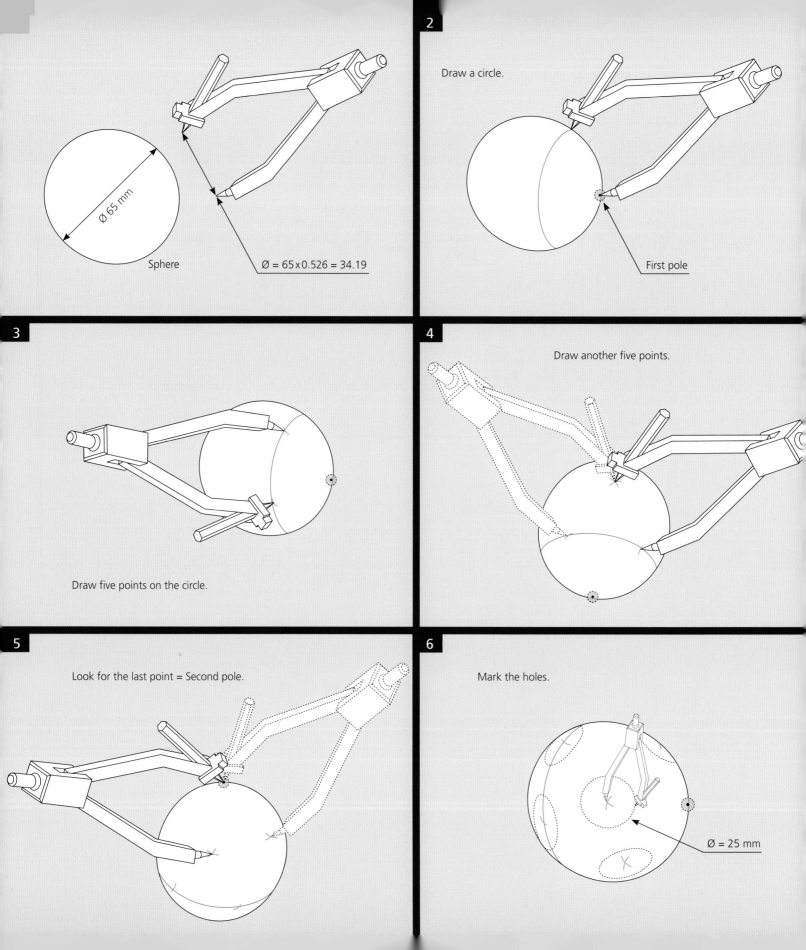

1

Ø 65 mm

Sphere

Ø = 65 × 0.526 = 34.19

2

Draw a circle.

First pole

3

Draw five points on the circle.

4

Draw another five points.

5

Look for the last point = Second pole.

6

Mark the holes.

Ø = 25 mm

The creation of Chinese spheres has fascinated woodturners all over the world for centuries. However, without tools that are made specifically for the size of the main sphere, this small masterpiece can't be created. Christian has developed a series of his own tools because he produces quite a few of these spheres. He sells them individually, or incorporates them into his larger pieces (see the gallery, page 200).

Important: In making Chinese spheres, you need to work with high precision. Both the turning of the sphere's diameter and the marking of the openwork must be done very precisely. First a sphere is turned as described with Project 1, *Sphere,* starting on page 35. The sphere must be absolutely round and have a diameter of exactly 65 mm.

It's difficult to photograph the marking process, so this part of the project is explained with drawings.

1__First, mark twelve equidistant points on the sphere. The factor to calculate this distance is 0.526. This factor is multiplied by the diameter of the sphere (65 mm). The result is 34.19 mm. This measurement is set on a pair of dividers.

2__Choose a point on the sphere as the first center point (first pole), and use the dividers to mark a circle around this pole.

3__On the resulting circle, choose any point and make an arc with the dividers that crosses this circle. This results in another point on the circle. Now place the dividers at this second point and make another arc. You will get a third point on the circle. Continue until you've marked five points on the circle. They must all be equidistant from each other.

4__From two points, each of which lie adjacent to each other on the circle line, mark intersections with the same divider setting. The result is five more points on the sphere.

5__From these new points, make arcs with the dividers. The twelfth and last point is marked.

6__Now, circles with a diameter of 25 mm are drawn around these twelve points. They mark the holes where the tools are applied. Once it's been prepared this way, the sphere can be turned.

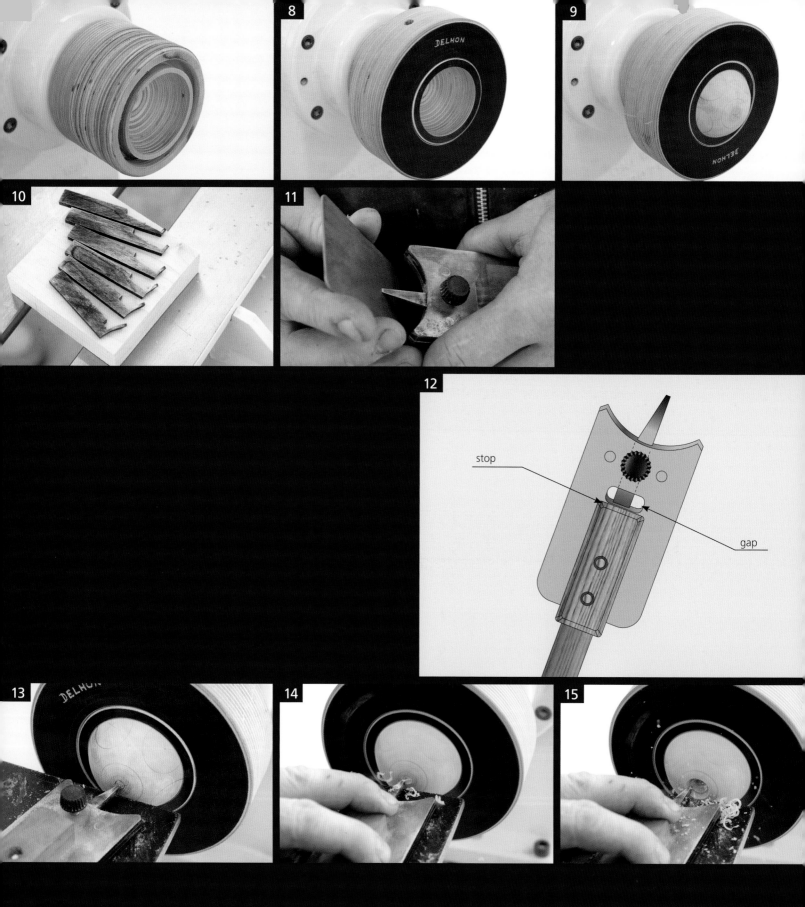

7__To do this, clamp it into a special chuck. The spherical chuck consists of two parts. The sphere is placed into the base body, which is screwed onto the spindle thread.

8__It is held in place by a ring-shaped lid, which is screwed onto the base body.

9__Clamp the sphere so that one of the twelve marked points lies centered inside the ring-shaped lid. For precise centering, use the tailstock.

Important: Precise work is essential for success!

10__For our Chinese sphere consisting of five spheres inside of each other, these are the tools to be used. On the far right is a narrow and straight steel that provides space for the following tools. The five angled steels are used consecutively for the individual spheres. Moving from right to left, they're used on the smallest to the largest sphere. Each one of these steels is inserted into the support up to the stop and fixed with a screw. The steels are of different lengths, so they disappear into the support at different lengths. This results in the various diameters of the individual spheres.

11__The first tool used is the straight steel, which is inserted into the tool support. It serves to make space so that the angled steels can be inserted later on. Each steel must be very sharp. If required, they can be sharpened with a diamond file (a small one is shown here).

12__A gap is located in front of the wooden handle. At this point you can control whether the tool is clamped to its stop. Make sure that no chips are inside the support, since that might prevent the complete insertion of the steel.

13__Set the horizontal table of the tool rest so that the steel cuts exactly at the height of the axis, and push the steel into the wood at the center until a small hole is created.

14__Enlarge the diameter with pulling cuts toward the left and deepen the hole.

15__Toward the outside, cut no deeper than up to the pencil mark. Toward the inside, a cone-shaped groove should be created.

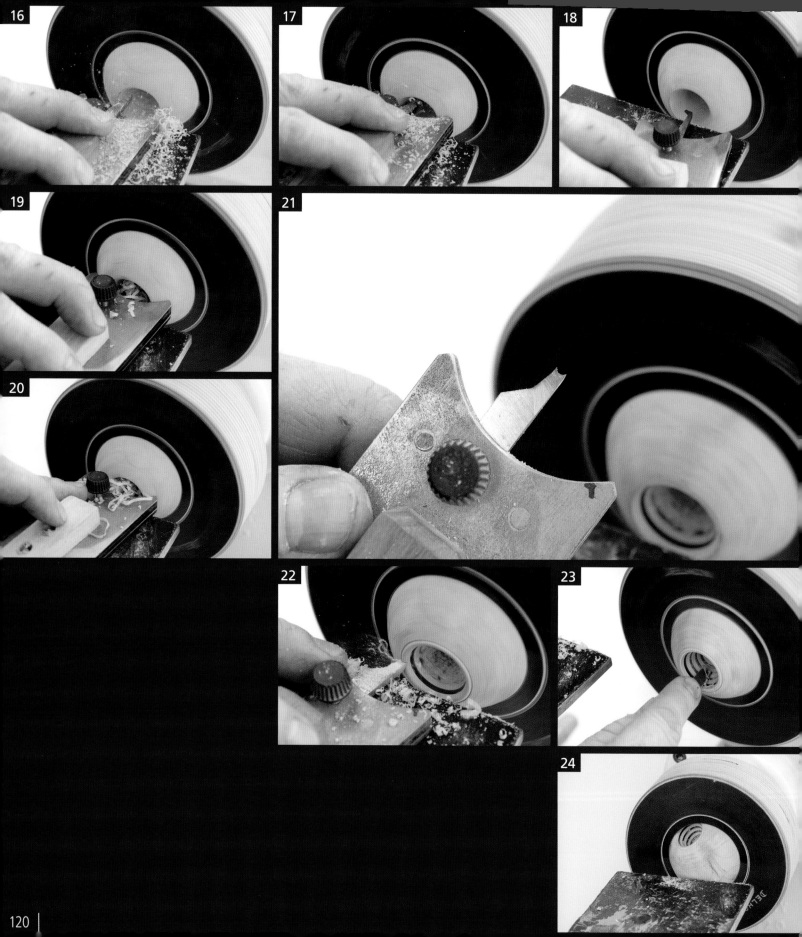

16__Work slowly into the depth . . .

17__ . . . until the curve of the tool support touches the sphere. The tool has now reached its maximum depth. The surface should be cut as cleanly as possible. The cone can be sanded.

18__Now clamp the tool for the smallest sphere into the support.

19__Carefully advance with the tool until the curve of the tool support touches the sphere. The angled steel should not yet touch the wood.

20__Keep the contact between the sphere and the support and guide the steel with small movements to the left into the wood. Continue to remove the shavings from the hole so the tool will not become stuck and so that you sense when the small "nose" of the steel has cut until its stop (no more shavings are produced).
Important: Apply slight pressure and make only small shavings.

Repeat this process consecutively with the other four sphere tools. The different lengths of the tools determine the diameters of the spheres.
Important: The position of the sphere in the spherical chuck is **not** changed!

21__After using the five spherical tools, Christian adds a small decoration at the edge of the opening. For this purpose he has made a small profiled steel, which cuts a rod into the wood.

22__This tool is not included with the spherical tool kit. One alternative is to keep the opening without decoration; or you could use the skew or a very fine gouge.

23__Sand the interior surface with a small rolled-up piece of abrasive paper.
Important: Make sure the abrasive paper doesn't become stuck in the hollow spaces.

24__Now loosen the sphere in the chuck and turn it to the next face to be worked on. Again, align the center of the opening with the tailstock and set the tool table so that the tool cuts directly at the center.

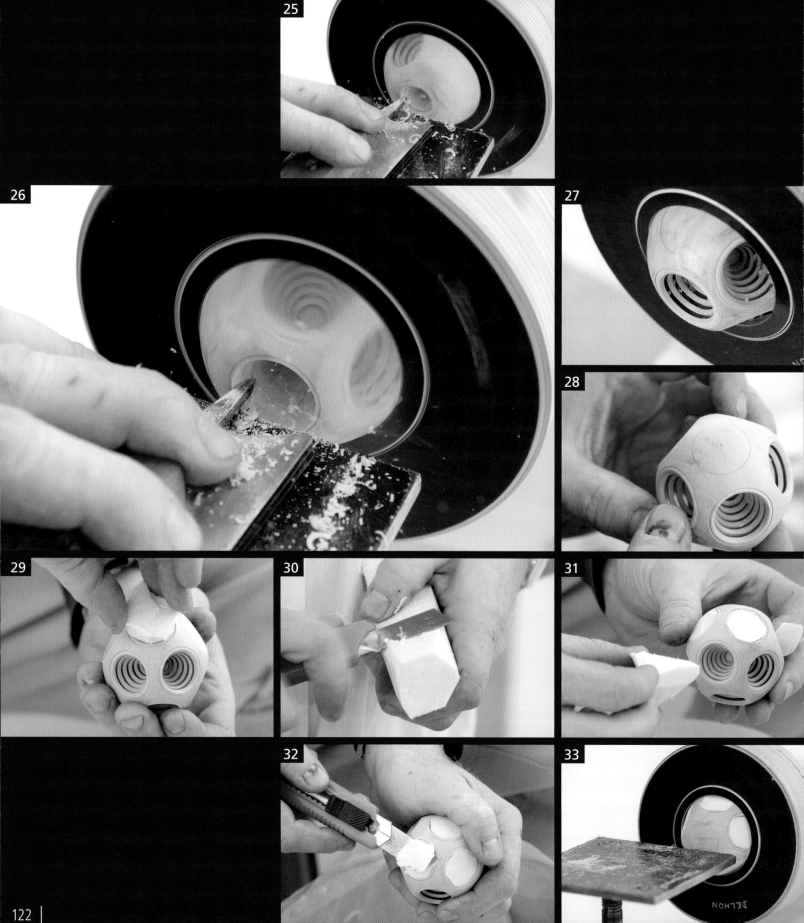

25__First use the straight cutter again to create the cone-shaped opening. Then repeat the steps shown in photos 13 to 20.

26__**Important:** Keep in mind that the piece becomes more delicate with each worked opening. So the tools should be used with increasing care and always with very little pressure. To keep them performing well, you need to sharpen the cutters regularly; a diamond file is best.

27__The plywood chuck provides a secure hold on the sphere without leaving pressure marks on the surface.

28__Before working the last point, remove the sphere from the chuck. The interior already shows the openwork from one cone to the other. The individual spheres, however, are still connected at various places. They become free only after the last face has been worked.

29__Before the last opening is created, secure the sphere segments. Christian used insulation material from a building supplier. It's soft yet stable, can be easily worked, and doesn't leave marks on the wood surface.

30__Sharpen the material into a conical shape . . .

31__ . . . and carefully push it into the openings.

32__Remove excess material so it's flush with the surface. Otherwise, the sphere can't be properly clamped into the chuck.

33__Then clamp the sphere into the chuck again, and align it for working the last face.

34__The straight steel once again creates space for using the spherical tools.

35__The resulting cone shows the small faces that still hold the individual spheres together.

36__After the last cutter is used, the spheres are no longer connected to each other. Only the plastic material keeps them in place.

37__Carefully remove the plastic cones by screwing a screw or a drill into the material. By pulling lightly, you can remove the material through the openings.

38__Now the five spheres are free and can be shifted against each other.

39__Sand the surface of the sphere. Christian has glued a leather disc with a diameter of about 15 cm onto a small plywood board. The leather disc has Velcro on it to hold sanding discs. During sanding, the leather disc gives a little and fits the curves of the pieces very nicely.

40__He sands with the leather disc using 1000 grit . . .

41__ . . . and then polishes with three abrasive mops and the appropriate waxes. The discs are attached to the chuck or to a special pin that is put onto the spindle. They're used consecutively with specific waxes. First comes a cotton disc with brown polishing paste: this makes for a very finely sanded surface. Then, a cotton disc with white polishing wax (Tripoli) is used, and this results in an extremely fine surface. Last is a flannel disc with carnauba wax. This hard wax protects the surface and gives it a shiny appearance.

42__Using light pressure against the polishing discs, the surfaces of the following two spheres are reached too. However, you should block them with your fingers so the delicate structures aren't flung around by the polishing machine.

43__The Chinese sphere is now sanded and polished.

If you need more of a challenge, there is also a special tool kit available for Chinese spheres with seven spheres.

Boxwood
Dia. 6.5 cm

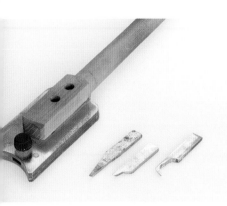

13___STAR IN SPHERE

CHRISTIAN DELHON

Materials	
Tools	Special tool kit for star in sphere with support
	Basic tool kit
	Spindle gouge
Wood	Boxwood
Accessories	Spherical chuck by Christian Delhon
	Hand and tool rest with horizontal table
	Calipers
	Dividers
	Sanding pad

1

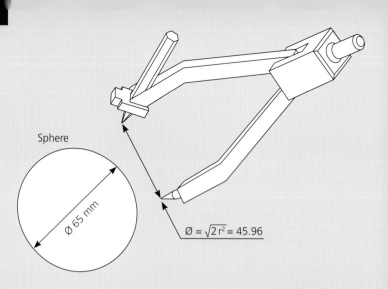

Sphere

Ø 65 mm

$Ø = \sqrt{2\,r^2} = 45.96$

2

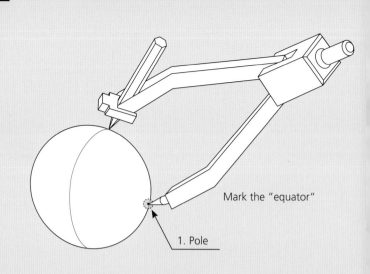

Mark the "equator"

1. Pole

3

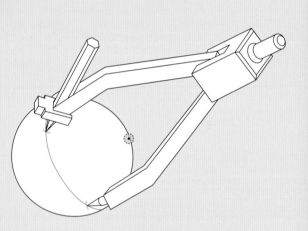

Mark the four points on the equator.

4

From the equator, determine the second pole.

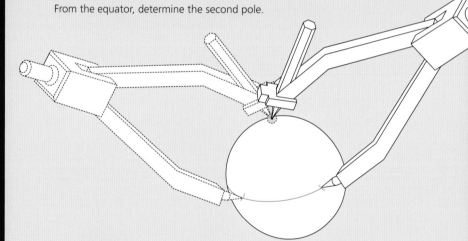

5

Mark circles with a diameter of 25 mm around the six points.

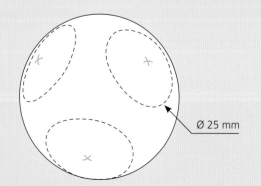

Ø 25 mm

6

You can determine the position of the small holes from the large holes.

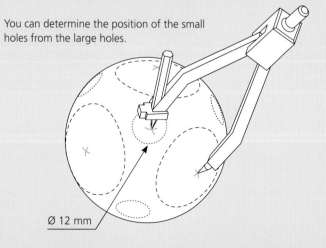

Ø 12 mm

This project, where a star-shaped object can be moved freely inside of a sphere, is a challenge that calls for precise workmanship and patience. Once again, it requires special tools. However, in this case, it only requires two steels that are affixed to the tool support.

First, make a precise sphere, as described in Project 1, *Sphere,* starting on page 35. Its diameter must be exactly 65 mm.

For the star inside the sphere, we need six large and, on the faces between them, small openings on the sphere. They are marked as follows:

1__To begin, six points must be marked on the sphere, equidistant from each other. Set the dividers to 45.96 mm.

2__Choose a point on the sphere as the first center point (first pole) and mark a circle around this pole, to obtain the equator.

3__Punch the dividers onto the equator and mark an arc (with the same measurement). You'll get a second point on the circle. Now set the dividers into this second point and mark another arc. You get a third point on the circle. Continue until you get to the first point on the equator. If it doesn't work out, it's because the dividers were not set precisely. Increase or decrease the setting you used and make new arcs, until all the points are equidistant.

4__Make arcs from these four points on the equator. The second pole becomes apparent.

5__Circles with a diameter of 25 mm are now marked around these six points. They indicate the holes where the tools will be used.

6__You can geometrically determine the position of the small holes using the points of the large holes. Circles with a diameter of 12 mm are marked around the centers of the small holes.

With this preparation done, the sphere can now be turned.

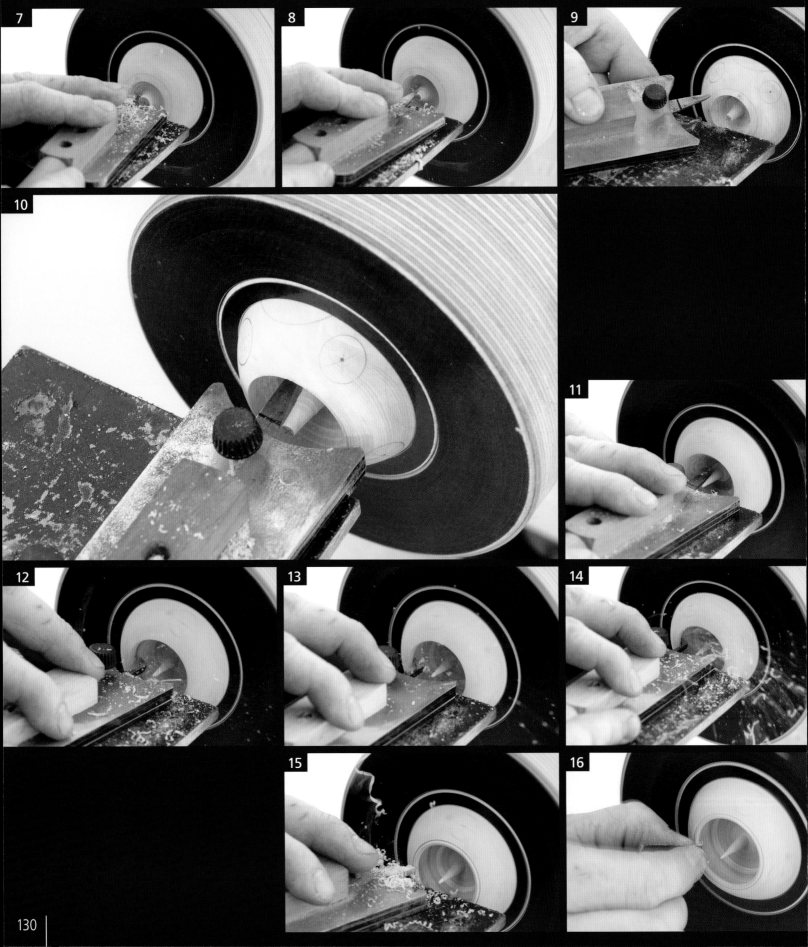

Clamp the sphere into the spherical chuck and align it precisely with the tailstock. Now we can start using the special tools.

7__First the straight steel is clamped into the tool support up to its stop. The tool support is placed onto the flat tool rest and the cutter is positioned somewhat to the left of the center.
Important: No material at the very center should be removed because later on one of the tips of the star will be at this spot.

8__Remove sliver after sliver with slight pressure, working out the tip.
Important: Make sure that the tip runs cone-shaped toward the inside.

9__Christian has added a mark to the cutter. It's used as a depth limiter and determines the size of the cube that will later be created in the center of the star.

10__Remove the material until the tip of the star reaches the marked line on the steel. At the same time, enlarge the diameter of the opening up to the pencil marking.

11__The cutting tool must be very sharp on both sides—first, to allow you to work with little pressure, and second, because this makes for clean cutting of the surface.

12__Now use the angled steel. It creates space at the lateral sides, and the sphere inside is undercut.

13__The steel cuts on both sides. So it can be used to remove material both laterally and into the depth.

14__The cutting edge is guided over the wood with small swaying movements to the left and right, and the first face of the cube is created.

15__To accent the opening, Christian once again adds a small groove to the edge of the opening. He's fabricated a fine steel, which can also be clamped to the tool support. However, experienced turners can create this small decoration with the skew or a very fine gouge.

16__Using a small piece of abrasive paper (without pressure!), the tip of the star and the face of the cube are sanded, and—as far as possible—the interior is sanded.

17__After sanding, the sphere is loosened inside the chuck and turned over so that the next face can be worked. **Important:** Align the sphere with the tailstock.

18__The steps are now repeated for each face, as described on page 131, photos 7 to 16.

19__ **Important:** Make sure that the tips of the stars are of the same size and of an even conical shape. You need to check the length of the tip, and its diameter at the cube.

20__ **21**__ **22**__

The photos clearly show the individual tips and faces that make up the cube-shaped body of the star. It's still connected to the sphere at various places and can't be moved freely.

23__Before the last face can be worked, the sphere is removed from the chuck. The star must now be locked in place so it won't come loose in an uncontrolled way during this last step. Christian uses insulation material here, just as he did in Project 12. It can be easily worked with a knife and shaped so that it fits into the openings of the sphere.

24__Push the prepared piece straight onto the tip of the star, very carefully so it doesn't break off.

25__Cut back the excess insulation material so it doesn't protrude out from the surface of the sphere.

26__You can clearly see that the star is still connected to the sphere on the right side. At this location the surface is not open. The other sides are already perforated and filled with insulation material.

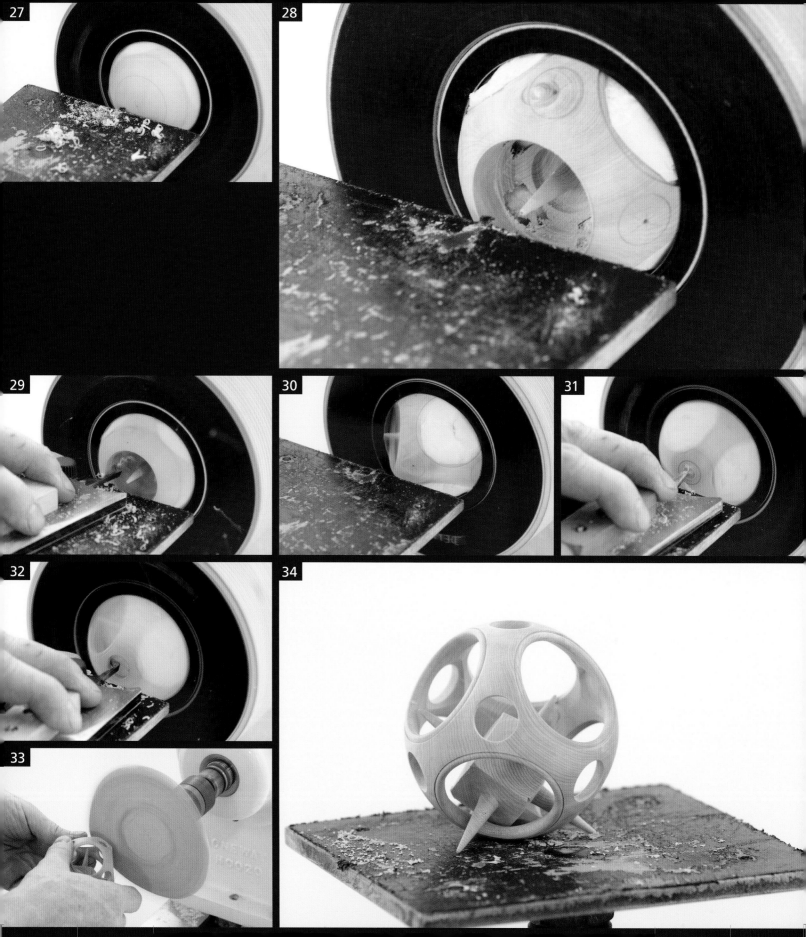

27__The sphere is clamped into the chuck once again and aligned for working the last face.

28__When working at the tip of the star, you can see the first open faces.

29__Using the angled cutter, the star is finally freed. After this last step at the star, sand the surface as you did with the previous openings.

30__For the small openings, the sphere is turned over inside the chuck so that the appropriate surfaces can be worked. These openings are meant as decoration, but through these windows the relatively large surfaces between the main openings can be cleanly undercut.

31__First, they are perforated with the straight steel . . .

32__ . . . then undercut with the angled steel. Once all of the small openings are done the sphere is taken out of the chuck. The insulation material can be removed with a screw or a drill; don't screw into the center, rather, screw alongside the tips of the stars, and then carefully pull out the insulation. The star can now be moved inside the sphere. If the interior diameter of the sphere is larger than the distance between two opposing star tips, the star can be turned completely inside of the sphere.

33__Finally, sand and polish the surface of the sphere. Christian uses the leather disc and polishing disc as described in Project 12, *Chinese Sphere,* on page 125, photos 39 to 42.

34__The sphere with the captured star is finished.

Ash
Dia. 4 cm
H 46 cm

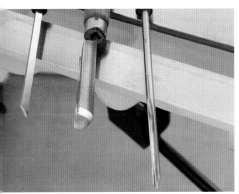

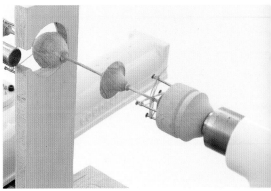

14___TREMBLEUR

JEAN-FRANÇOIS ESCOULEN

Materials	
Tools	Roughing gouge, 19 mm
	Bedan parting tool, 5 mm
	Spindle gouge, 9 mm
Wood	Ash, 35 x 35 x 500 mm
	Important: The wood must be sawed in such a way that the fibers are parallel to the axis of rotation. No oblique cut; no shortened fibers!
Accessories	Steady rest with centering rollers
	Auxiliary steady rest, self-built
	Waxed thread (available at art supply stores or shoe repair shops)

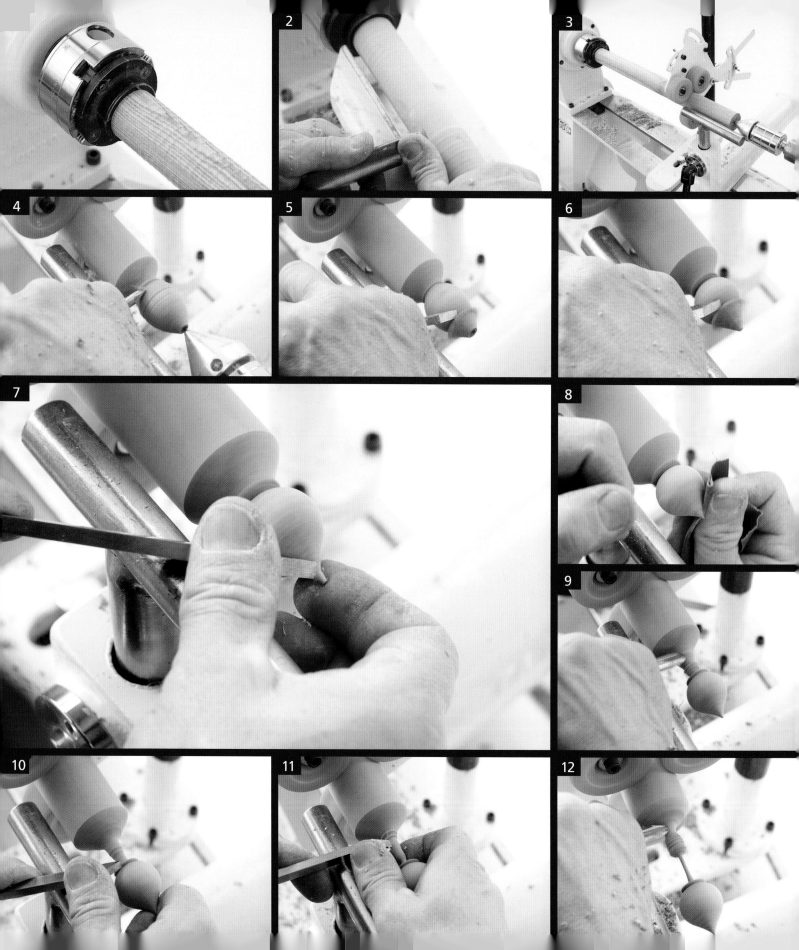

Traditionally, trembleurs (probably from the French *trembler*, "to shake") were pieces of artistic woodturning that challenged the craftsmanship of the turner. The variety and delicacy of the lined-up profiles and, in particular, the extremely thin sections between the profile sections were, and remain, a challenge for the turner. Since these filigreed tremblers are obviously very delicate, they are usually displayed in glass tubes. (However, one of Jean-François's trembleurs posed a problem in terms of finding the right tube, since that masterpiece—made from a single piece of ebony—is taller than he is!)

1__The ash piece is planed and clamped into the chuck with a stud (in this case, the talon chuck).

2__Once inside the chuck, the piece is turned over, once again, and treated with a finishing cut.

3__To turn the drop-shaped tip of the trembleur, use the steady rest. It must be aligned so that the long piece runs with the axis without being supported by the tailstock. The head of the steady rest can be adjusted in terms of its height and set to the axis. Three rotating plastic rollers, which can be adjusted to the diameter of the round rod, stabilize the rotating blank.

4__First, work out the drop shape of the tip with the help of the rotating tip. For this Jean-François uses the spindle gouge.

5__To remove the hole of the tip and to shape the details, he uses the bedan. It's similar to our parting tool, but is used for many other tasks; Jean-François also uses it for cutting, profiling, and structuring.

6__This photo clearly shows how the bedan is used as a skew . . .

7__ . . . and even concave shapes, such as here for the fine tip, are no problem for the bedan due to its narrow width.

8__The profile of the tip is now completed, and is sanded to the desired grit (in this case, 180 to 400).

9__Using the spindle gouge, the next profile section is prepared.
Important: Work with a small sliver and little pressure.

10__The bedan is perfectly suited for working the small plate that separates the drop-shaped tip from the thin connecting rod. In order for this section and the following thin sections to not break off you should observe the following:

11__**Important:** The thin sections should not be turned along their full length, but instead divided into several sections (about 15 to 20 mm each).

12__Starting from the right, these sections are consecutively turned down to their final size. The spindle gouge is well-suited to remove material, and the bedan can be used to smooth the surface.

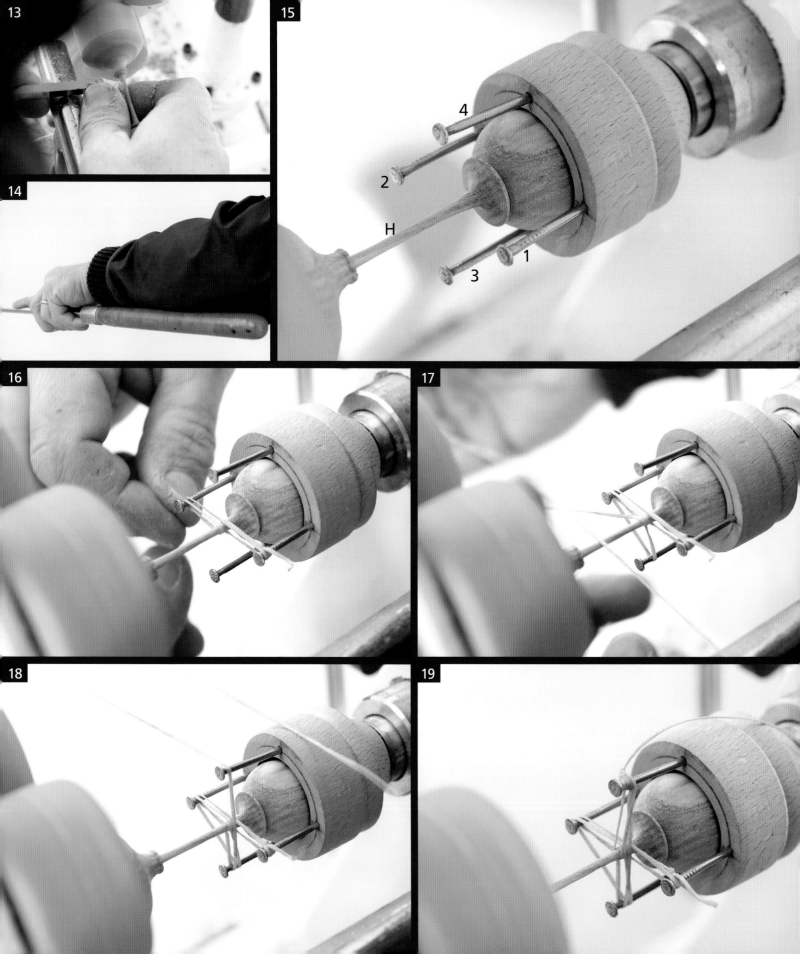

13__**Important:** Support the piece with your hand to equalize the pressure of the tool. The thin connecting section is also sanded to the desired gauge.

14__To be able to smoothly and safely guide the tools on the profiles in small sections, Jean-François places them against his forearm. This allows him to guide the tool with one hand while the other supports the piece.

15__The tip must be stabilized before working the next section. This is done with a homemade wooden chuck. A conical stud is turned onto the wooden chuck and placed into the tailstock. The body of the chuck is hollowed out so that the tip of the trembleur fits into it **without** touching the chuck since the chuck will not rotate along with it (this is difficult to show clearly with photographs)! Jean-François has marked a line on the front edge of the wooden chuck where four nails are hammered in so that they form a precise square.

16__A waxed thread is looped around the piece. It's quite strong, and the waxed surface allows the piece to slide inside the thread without creating burn marks.

Tying the chuck: Tie the thread to nail 1 and loop it around H back to 1. Around 1 to 2. Around 2 to H, around H to 2.

17__Around 2 to 3, around 3 to H, around H to 3.

18__Around 3 to 4, around 4 to H, around H to 4.

19__Tie the thread at 4. This way, the piece is held equidistant from the nails and it's stabilized in all four directions.

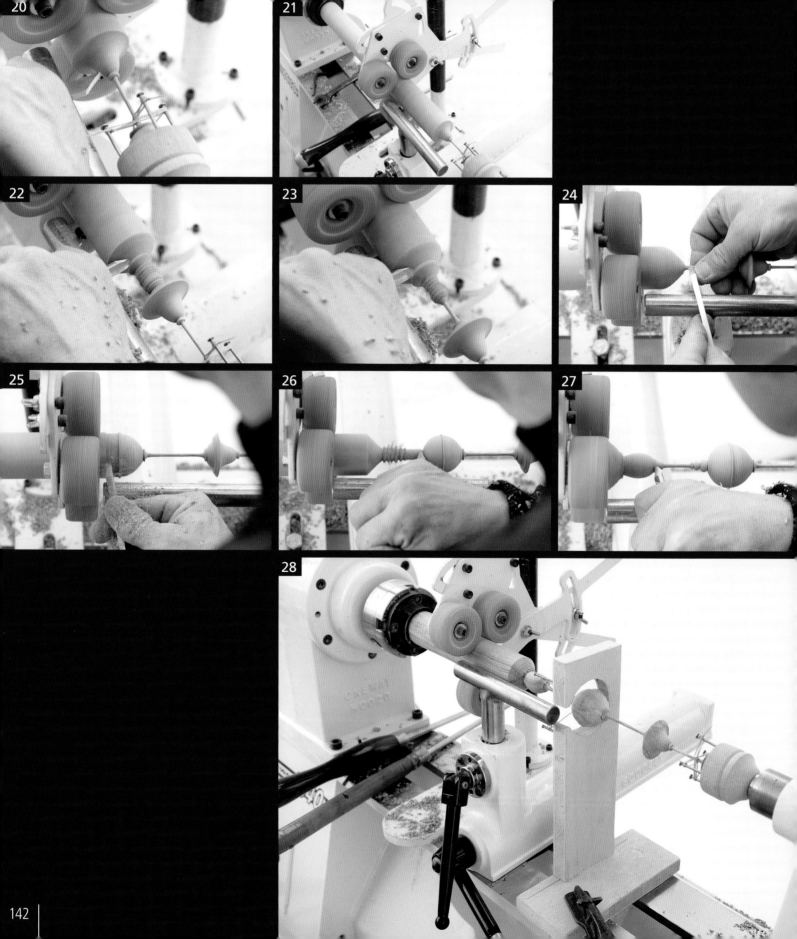

20__Now the work at the next profile can be done. The material is removed with a spindle gouge, and the bedan is used for the details.

21__The steady rest is shifted to the left on the bed to make room for the next work steps.

22__The left side of the profile is created and the next thin section is prepared.

23__Work again section by section, to the final size . . .

24__ . . . and clean up the surface with the bedan.

25__The next profile is prepared with the help of the steady rest, and the right side is completed.

26__After shifting the steady rest, there's sufficient space to make the left side of the profile and the next section. Proceed as described above, and sand the finished sections.

27__The fourth profile falls at about the center of the piece. Even rotation is provided by the steady rest.

28__For the next section the steady rest must be repositioned. To keep the trembleur supported an auxiliary steady rest is used. It can be fabricated from MDF. It stands on the bed and is affixed with a clamp. The vertical plate has an opening at the height of the axis, which is used to push the auxiliary steady rest over the piece.

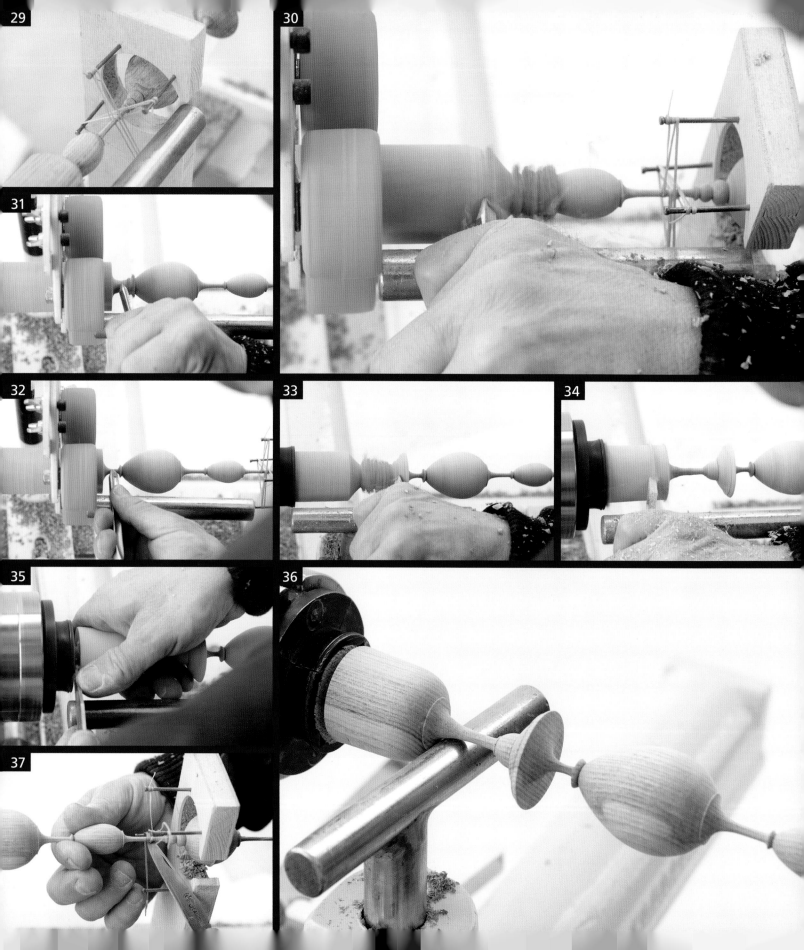

29__ On the left side of the plate, four nails are attached the same way as on the wooden chuck that was placed into the tailstock.

30__ Waxed thread is used again for stabilization. This allows for finishing the left side of the fourth profile. **Important:** In making longer trembleurs, several of these auxiliary steady rests are used, and are attached to a section at a distance of about 15 to 20 cm.

31__ Now the fifth profile is worked, and is once again connected to the previous one by a thin section.

32__ All of the profiles begin and end with a small plate or with a notch, in order to clearly define beginning and end.

33__ Because we'll be working close to the chuck, the steady rest is not required for stabilization.

34__ The last profile and the foot are turned with the spindle gouge and the bedan.

35__ The trembleur is carefully cut off. Inexperienced turners should only cut back up to a small stud, and then use a saw (Japanese saw) for the rest.

36__ Tip: The trembleur is still clamped into the wood chuck (on the tailstock side) and the auxiliary steady rest. Therefore, place the piece onto the tool rest . . .

37__ . . . until you've severed the waxed thread. This keeps the delicate piece from breaking.

Curly maple
Dia. 25 cm
H 6 cm

15____ECCENTRIC BOWL

JEAN-FRANÇOIS ESCOULEN

Materials	
Tools	Bowl gouge, 9 mm
Wood	Curly maple, diameter 270 mm
	Veneer carrier, diameter ca. 12 cm
Accessories	Eccentric chuck, Escoulen No. 3
	Superglue or PVC glue
	Danish oil

Jean-François told me that at first he, too, had a hard time predicting what the result would be when a piece is taken out of axis in a certain way. But, with each piece he created, his experience increased and his experiments with eccentric woodturning resulted in lots of new ideas that he wanted to turn into reality. Since the greatest problem wasn't coming up with the ideas, but the limitations of clamping a piece, he developed his own chucks.

This project is a good one for trying eccentric woodturning with cross-grain wood. The chuck offers a wealth of possibilities (see the information in the "Equipment" section, pages 24 and 25) and at the same time it lets you work without risking injury.

1__Screw the faceplate of the eccentric Escoulen chuck onto a wooden disc sawed to the right size. This disc, made from scrap wood, lets you take advantage of the entire height of the curly maple blank.

2__Plane the blank if necessary, to prepare a large enough flat surface to glue the wooden disc to. Use PVA or superglue.

3__Align all of the moving parts of the chuck body with the axis, and fix it in place.

4__Now clamp the faceplate, onto which the piece is attached, into the chuck. The rotating tip in the tailstock is stabilized from the right.

5__Using the bowl gouge, first work the bottom side of the bowl. Align the tool rest accordingly.

6__Make the cuts from the edge to the bottom at first, because the tool removes material more effectively in this direction. With regard to the surface quality, however, this is the wrong cutting direction since it runs against the grain.

7__So the last cuts need to be done with the grain, from the bottom to the edge. Jean-François uses the bowl gouge with a pulling cut.

Important: The tool must be well-sharpened.

8__If the wood is very porous and fibrous, as in this case, you can stabilize the surface with a primer (in this case, sanding sealer) before the last cuts. This keeps the fibers from moving away and allows for cutting them cleanly.

9__Finally, make the last cuts, with a very fine sliver.

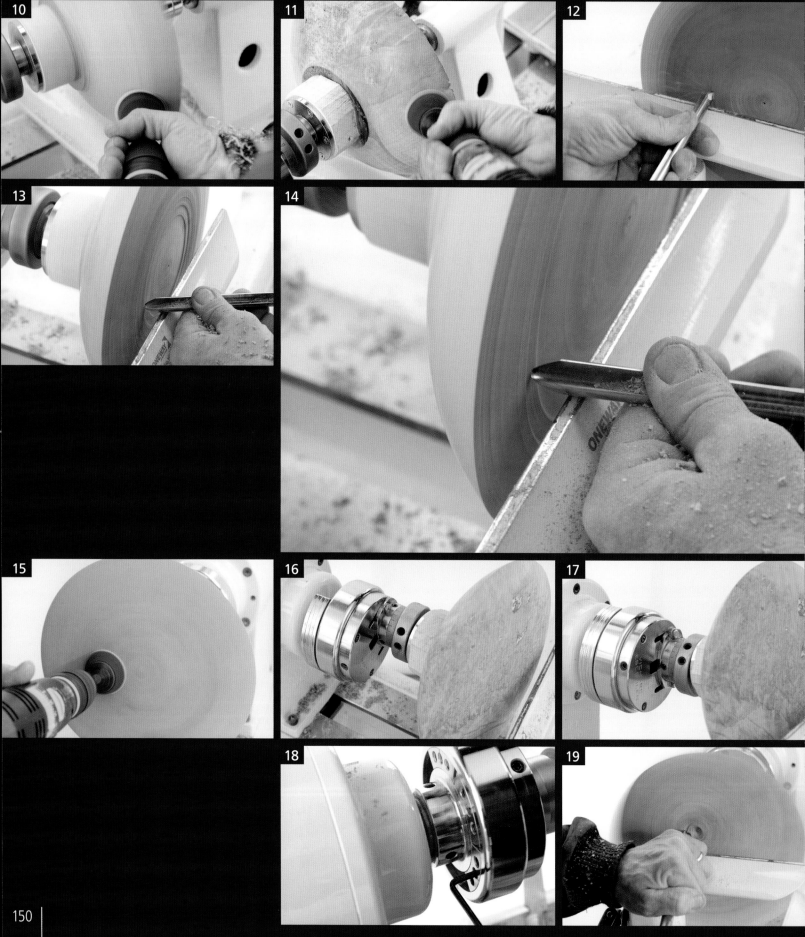

10__Sand the surface with a sanding pad chucked into a cordless drill.

 Tip: To do this, reduce the rotation speed of the lathe, and of the drill.

11__You can work particularly difficult sections with the turned-off lathe.

12__Now we turn to the top side of the bowl. First, turn the surface flat and remove the saw cut.

13__Since the top side should feature a slight concavity, make the cuts from the inside toward the edge (in the case of grooves, from the edge to the center).

14__Set the bezel of the gouge and make fairly long cuts.

15__After the hollow is done, sand the surface.

16__Now the opening of the bowl must be shifted toward the outside and lie tilted inside the chuck body. So shift the part of the chuck to which the faceplate is attached, laterally.

17__Then tilt the faceplate inside the chuck.

 Important: During your first attempts you shouldn't use much of a lateral shift and angle. Approach the process carefully!

18__The eccentric chuck features counterweights on the back of the chuck body. They must be set so that the imbalance that's created by changing the chuck is canceled out or at least significantly reduced.

19__You can clearly see where the new center lies, and how much the blank rotates to one side.

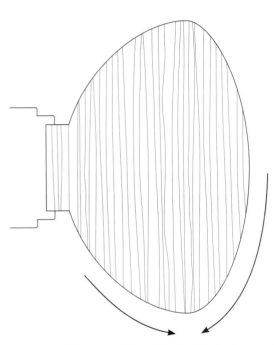

Always work from the short to the long grain.

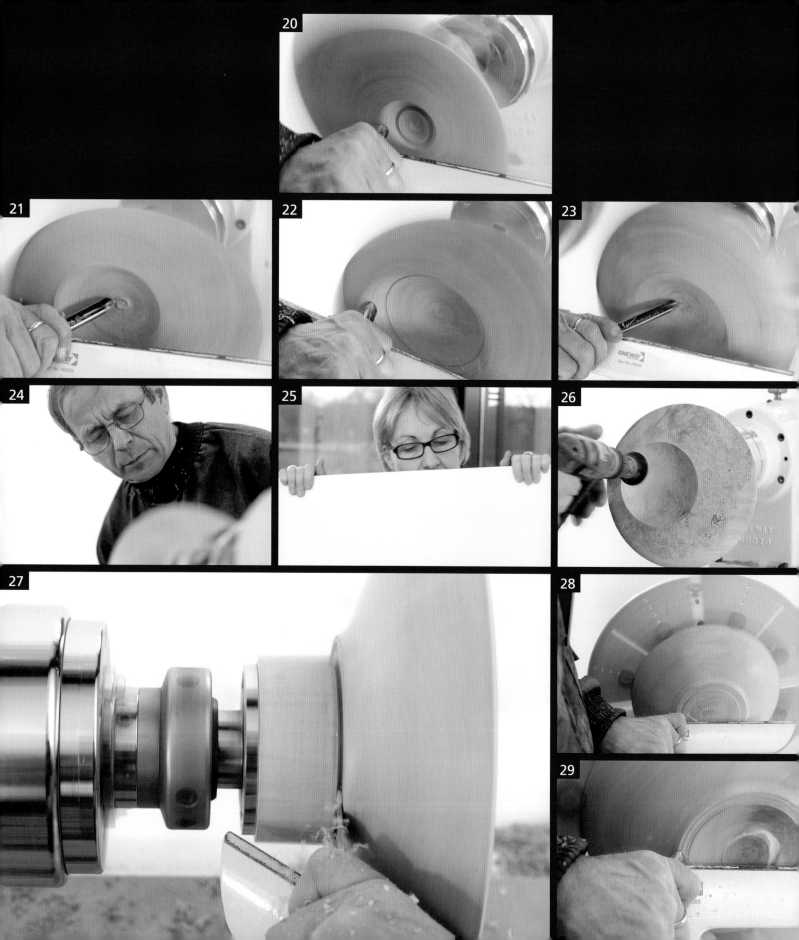

20__By tilting, the tool reaches the new protruding areas earlier than the lower-lying ones. This effect is increased by the curved surface of the bowl.

21__Work with the abutting bezel from the outside toward the inside—that is, with the grain.

22__When changing the setting of the tool rest, make sure that the piece can turn freely . . .

23__ . . . and that your fingers don't get into the area of the rotating blank.

24__ 25__
While Jean-François works with high concentration, I try to "capture" the light . . . .

26__Sand the cavity with the sanding pad; work difficult areas using the turned-off lathe.

27__To finish the bowl, the chuck is aligned with the axis and the tool rest is placed to the left side. Using a narrow parting tool, separate the bowl from the sample wood, leaving only a small stud. The stud is sawed off later.

Tip: When cutting off, work with overlapping cuts so there is enough space for the tool, to keep it from becoming stuck.

28__To further work the bottom side of the bowl, clamp it onto large aluminum clamps (mega jumbo jaws). The rubber-covered clamps hold the wood without damaging it.

29__Now the stud (and the remaining glue) can be removed and the bottom can be undercut. Sand the bottom, and finish the piece with several coats of Danish oil.

Important: Each coat of oil has to dry thoroughly (at least 4 to 6 hours) before you apply a new one.

Birch
W 36 cm
H 15 cm
L 40 cm

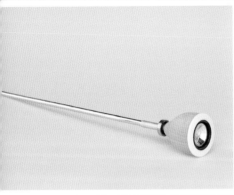
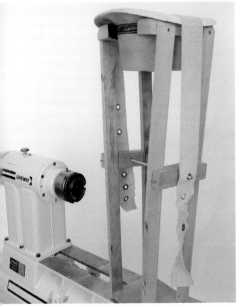
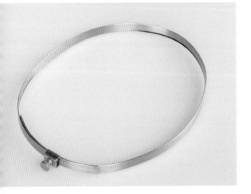

16___COWBOY HAT

ROLAND WALTER

Materials	
Tools	Bowl gouge, 9 mm
	Skew, 19 mm
Wood	Freshly cut birch, diameter ca. 40 cm
Accessories	Faceplate, 15 cm
	Hat chuck
	Light chuck
	Bender
	Head measurement band

155

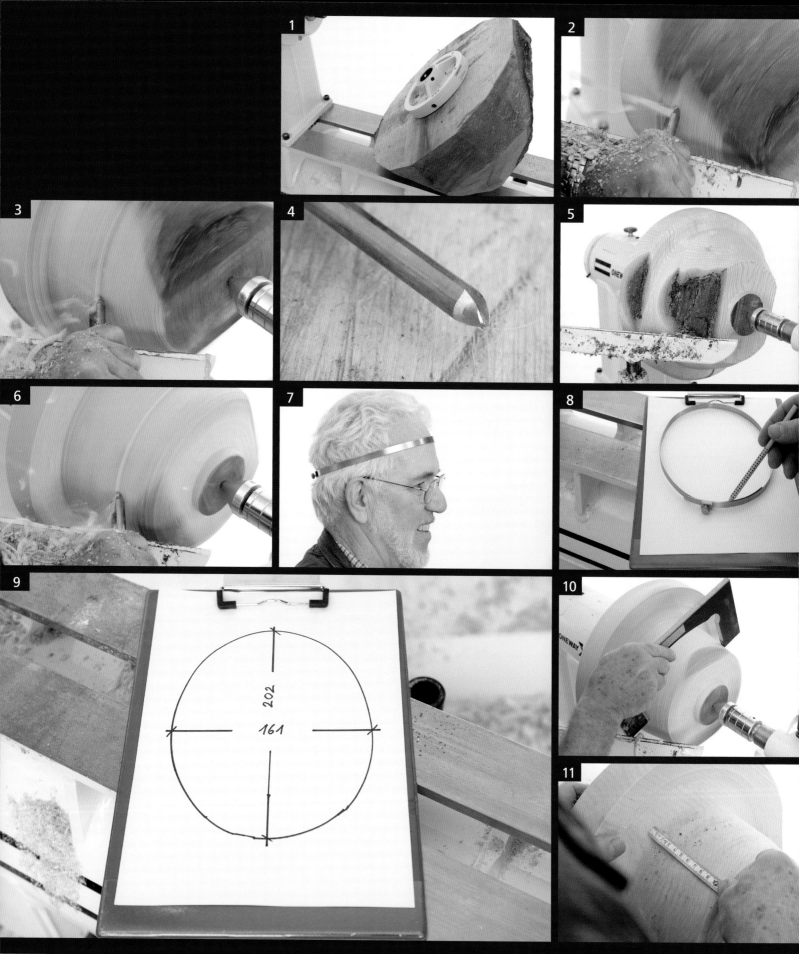

There's no doubt about it: if you're walking around with a wooden hat, you will not be ignored. These amaze on-lookers because the shape corresponds exactly to that of a felt or leather hat. But the color and grain leave no doubt about the material being wood. And if you think a wooden hat is heavy and uncomfortable to wear, you're about to learn otherwise. The fit and the comfort of these hats are on a par with those of their more ordinary relatives, particularly if you create a fit as masterful as Roland does.

1__Cut the wood blank as round as possible with the saw.
   Important: Make sure you don't remove too much material at the sides. You don't want the cone to be pointy, because that won't lead to a harmonious hat shape.
       Screw a faceplate onto the surface. It should be fairly stable since the moist blank is quite heavy. The faceplate used here (Oneway) is cast iron and has a diameter of 15 cm.

2__Place the blank onto the spindle, supported by the rotating tip. First turn the brim part round.

3__Then work the remaining material until all the surfaces left by the saw have disappeared. The moist wood can be worked easily, and the gouge lets you effectively remove the wood with a large sliver.

4__The bowl gouge (Oneway) features a V-shaped profile. This allows for grinding the sides all the way down. Contrary to the normal method, Roland has sharpened the main bezel with a crown. This round back allows for turning the tool easily. A second, narrow bezel results in a thin and sharp cutting edge that creates a great surface. The tool can be easily rolled on the round crown and allows for carefully approaching the very sharp blade. This is a major advantage for working the extremely thin walls of the hat.

5__Continue to stop the lathe to make sure that no pieces of bark or bast remain on the surface. They might fall off when drying so they need to be completely removed.

6__The section for the brim remains, with a height of about 4 cm. The bottom of the hat can keep a small stud around the rotating tip for now.

7__To make the hat the right size, Roland has made himself a copper band that can be adjusted in length with a screw. The band is placed around the head and adjusted.

8__A small screw allows for adjusting the head measurement to the right size. Then place the band on a piece of paper, and use a pencil to transfer the head shape to the paper.

9__Measure and mark the length and width of the oval.
   Important: Use the following formula to determine the correct interior hat diameter (to be turned) in mm:

$$\frac{length + width}{2} + 14 \text{ (shrinkage)} = \text{interior diameter}$$

In our example, this is:

$$\frac{202 + 161}{2} + 14 = \frac{363}{2} + 14 = 182 + 14 = 196\,mm$$

Tip: Add 2 to 4 mm for narrow head shapes.
       This formula takes into account the shrinkage of the wood, and gives the size of the initial interior diameter of the hat.

10__The outer diameter corresponds to the inner diameter plus 6 mm (2 x 3 mm wall thickness). Because Roland has turned many hats, he's made special templates out of MDF for the most common hat sizes. You can also check the measurement with calipers.

11__The height of the hat, measured from the brim, should be 105 to 120 mm. The measurement depends on the total size of the hat. Height and diameter should be of harmonious proportions.

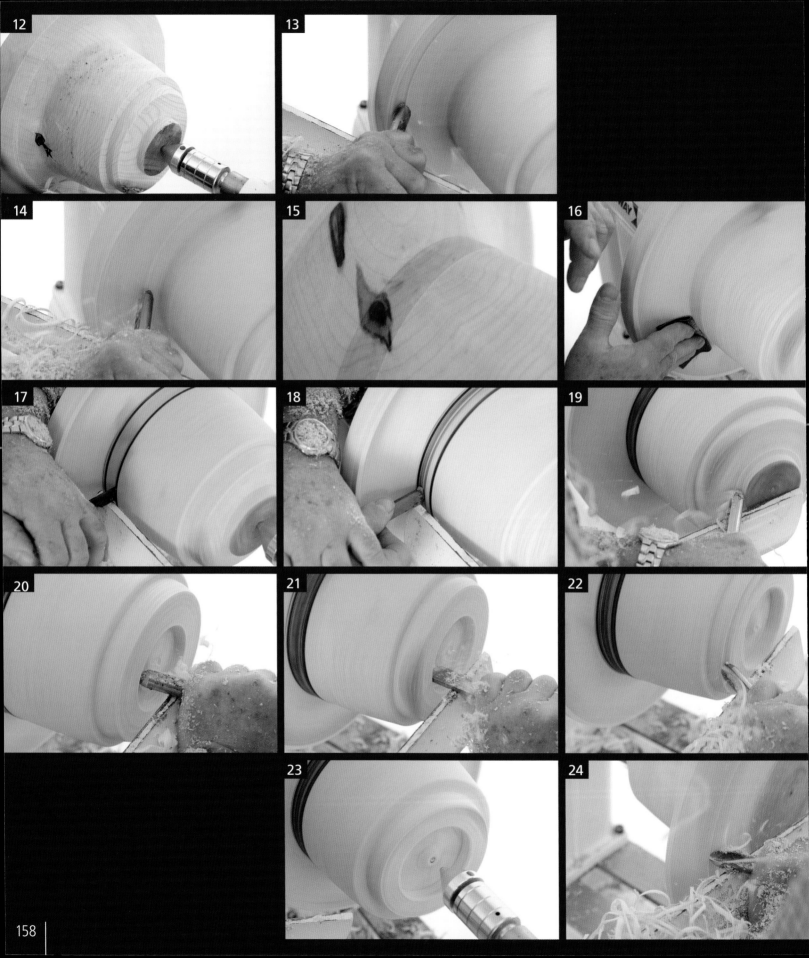

12__The protrusion visible on the right is not included in the measurement. This area will get a groove turned to it in order to rechuck the hat. The amount of tapering toward the top of the hat shape depends on the style of the hat and the personal taste of the woodturner (or the wearer). The surface at the height of the hatband remains cylindrical and slightly domed (0.5 to 1 mm).

13__Once the shape of the hat has been created, turn the curve of the brim. The correct cuts are from the center to the brim, and . . .

14__ . . . from the hatband to the center of the brim on the other side.

15__An "eye" mark, which appeared unexpectedly during our project, might be a nice highlight on the otherwise plain, light-colored wood. But with a spot like this you always run the risk that it may crack while drying, and especially while bending. So watch it carefully.

16__Once the outer side is finished, sand the surface. With moist wood you can certainly use coarser grits so the paper doesn't gum up as quickly. It doesn't make much sense to sand finely while the wood is wet. Grits of 240 to 320 are good enough for now.
Important: Make sure you sand cleanly and swiftly. The surface dries out quickly, and if the process takes too long cracks may appear.

17__Now mark the raised part of the hatband on both sides. Press a thin piece of ebony that's been sharpened at the end against the rotating blank until a black line becomes visible.

18__Mark the inner face of the hatband in the same way, using a lighter wood (like beech).

19__Next, remove the rotating tip and cut (turn) the stud off.

20__Cut a groove into the protruding material.

21__So the chuck will be well-affixed to this groove, work the edge with a skew chisel (depending on the shape of the chuck clamps).
Important: Allow the surface at the center of the groove to protrude slightly so the bottom of the hat can have a slightly concave shape.

22__**Important:** The bottom of the hat is worked to a width of 10 to 15 cm at the outer edge so that the wall thickness can later be checked with a light (see page 163, photo 49).

23__Before rechucking mark the center again with the rotating tip. This allows for retensioning where required and for realignment using the centering hole.

24__Fit the blank into the chuck.
Important: Make sure that the lathe is turning roundly. The thin wall doesn't allow for deviations.

Now the curve of the brim can be worked.

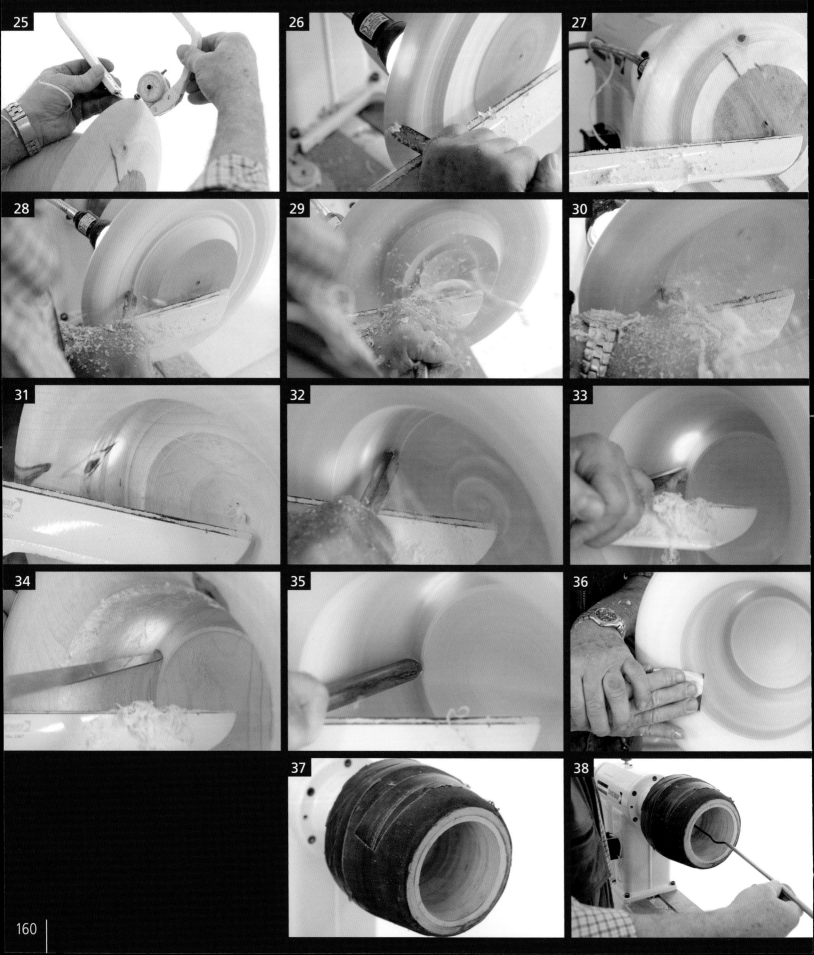

25__The wall thickness should be 3 mm. Roland has developed a special template for measuring both the brim and the wall of the hat.

26__The thinner the brim, the better the thickness of the material can be checked with light. If the light is even and of the same color at all areas, then the surface is of the same thickness.

27__The curve of the brim is done from the deepest point toward the outside, and worked to the same thickness at all areas.

28__Complete the curve toward the inside. Once again the light beam is used to control the wall thickness.

29__Remove the remaining cone with the bowl gouge . . .

30__ . . . and hollow the hat out.
Important: Abut the bowl gouge carefully, and make sure there's a harmonious transition from the brim into the inside of the hat.

31__When hollowing out you usually work with light.
Important: You need a source of strong light that won't produce too much heat.

32__The thin wall requires a secure abutting of the tool. Before each cut, place the crowned back of the bowl gouge onto the wood. Then roll the tool over carefully until the tip produces the sliver. This prevents an overly deep or uncontrolled cut on the thin wall.

33__Place the tool rest into the cavity. This way the tool will be supported even during the difficult cuts at the bottom of the hat—such as the curve.

34__The wall thickness from the brim to the curve at the hat's bottom must be as even and thin as possible. Roland checks the thickness (3 mm) with calipers. The photos show that he's reached the highest point and has already turned the transition to the hat's bottom.

35__Give the bottom a slightly concave curve. The tool must be carefully abutted to the edge.

36__Now you can sand the interior.
Important: Sand precisely, and swiftly. Apply only slight pressure!

37__To be able to rechuck the piece once again to work the bottom of the hat, Roland has created a "hat chuck." Its conical body, made of MDF, is hollowed out and has neoprene glued to it. This non-slip surface allows for chucking hats of different diameters. The hat chuck is perforated and has a groove on the back, which is used to clamp it into chuck.

38__The light chuck, which is now mounted to the interior of the hat chuck, is made up of a metal tube with a small wooden lampshade at its end containing a low-voltage lamp.

39__ The cable is run through the metal tube and put through the spindle. The diameter of a small ball bearing that is affixed to the end of the metal tube matches the bore of the hat chuck. This way the tube is guided inside of the hat chuck.

40__ In order for it to not rotate along with it, a pair of vise grips is affixed to the outside of the spindle. This assures that the tube and the lamp stay stable while only the small ball bearing rotates with the hat chuck.

41__ The lamp is connected to a low voltage transformer outside of the lathe and illuminates the hat chuck and the interior of the hat.

42__ The hat is now placed over the hat chuck and aligned with the rotating tip in the central hole.
Important: Check that the lathe turns roundly!

43__ We darkened the workshop to be able to clearly show the next steps. This lets you see the light at the bottom of the hat.

44__ to 51__
First remove the extra material around the groove and then—following the light—match the outer shape to the inner shape.

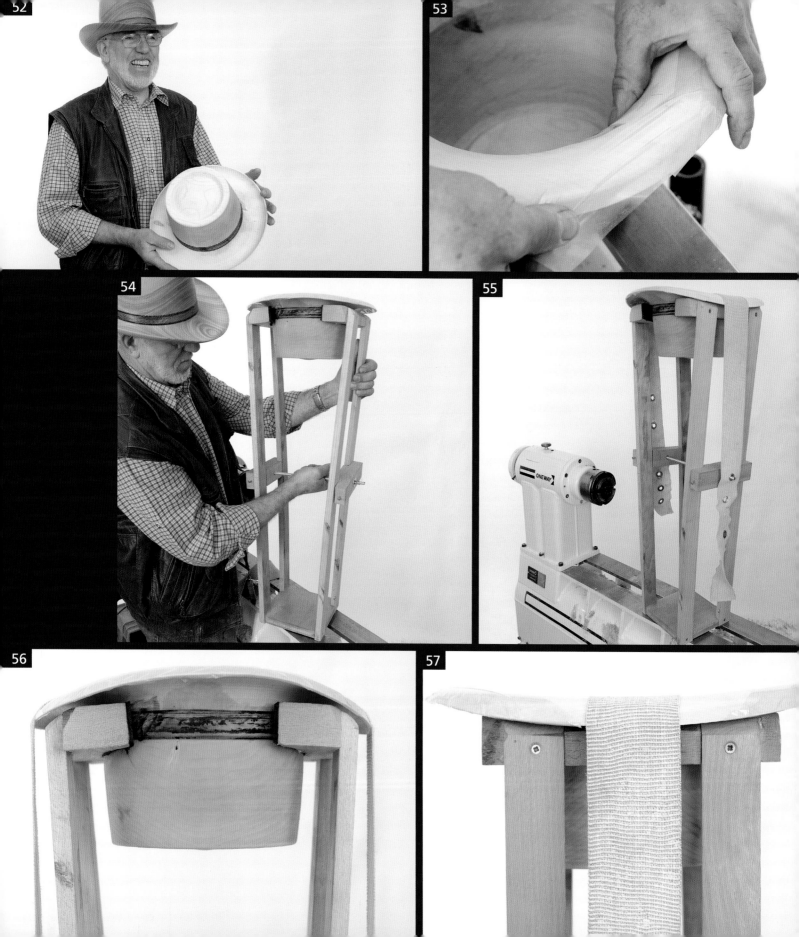

52__ The hat is finished now, and with its thin wall it's just as light as a hat made from leather or felt. However, it is still nearly round so it has to be fitted to the natural shape of the head.

53__ Secure both of the front ends of the hat with tautly stretched packing tape. The wood fibers are held together and don't run the risk of being pushed apart during the bending.

54__ Now clamp the hat into the bender. The wooden frame features an adjustable center section that can be moved up and down, and which pulls together the long rails. This provides the oval shape to the hat, with a more pronounced stretch than normally happens during the drying of the wood.

Tip: Start out with very little pressure at first and slowly increase it.

Important: The rails must be long so that a flexible pressure can be created.

55__ The brim of the hat is bent too. Roland used furniture-upholstery straps that feature eyelets, which are attached to the center section of the bender.

56__ The half-round rails are fitted with felt, and they cradle the hat without damaging it during the pressure.

57__ Bend the brim downward with the strap. This gives the characteristic cowboy-hat shape.

Important: The hat needs to be monitored, and perhaps adjusted, over several days. Regularly spray the front and back of the hat with water, especially during the first two days. Control the sideways pressure and readjust it if needed. The straps might also have to be adjusted. Observe whether any cracks are forming. You should immediately take care of them by glueing them with superglue.

When the shape no longer changes, you can assume that the hat is dry. Now it can be sanded again if needed. With colored or strongly grained woods, several layers of oil might be called for; with lighter woods, as in our project here, you might want to apply wax instead.

Curly maple
Dia. 30 cm
H 6 cm

17 ____BOWL—HALF OPEN

JO WINTER

Materials	
Tools	Bowl gouge, 9 mm
	Parting tool
	Woodpecker's beak
	Giraffe neck
Wood	Curly maple, diameter 30 cm, height 6 cm, planed if possible
Accessories	Sanding pad with cordless screwdriver or angle grinder
	Danish oil
	Sanding paper or pad
	Steel wool

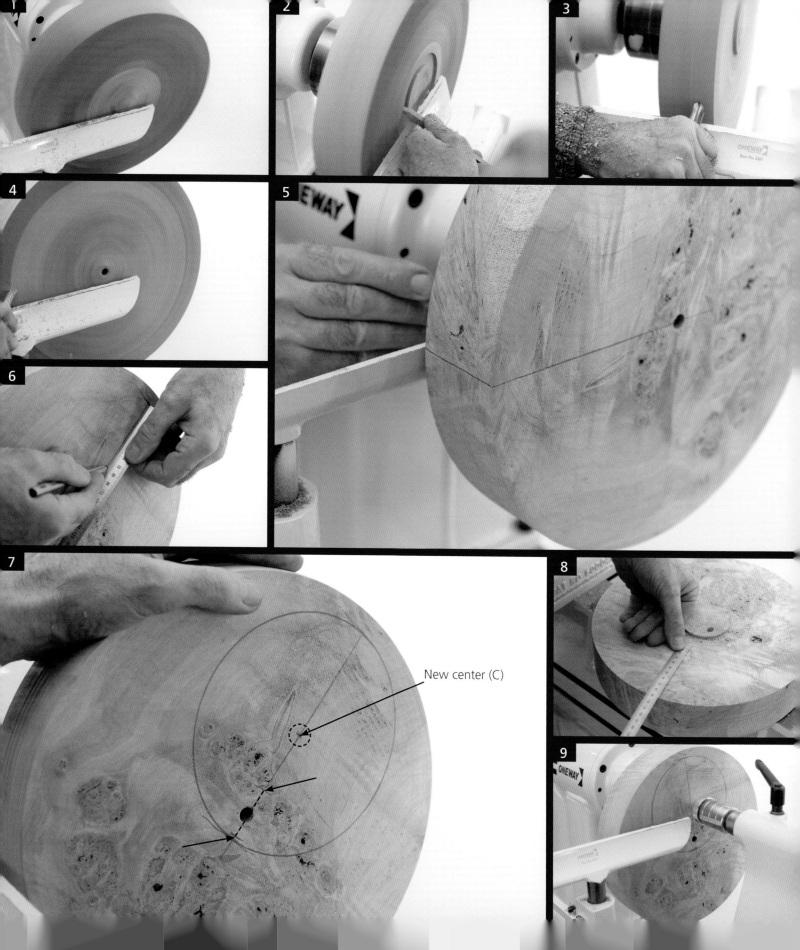

New center (C)

Jo has always been fascinated by non-round or eccentrically chucked pieces and their flying shadow, which gives the impression of a closed rotating body. He purposely incorporates edges or eccentrically-running surfaces into his creations. In this bowl, with a body that has been created with rotational symmetry, the opening is off center, but the bowl nevertheless is completely hollowed out—even under the closed surface!

1__Place the blank onto the screw inside of the chuck.
   Important: To enhance the grain of such a gorgeous blank, you have to carefully consider where the future top and bottom of the bowl will be located.
2__First turn the bottom side flat, and add a foot. Its diameter partly depends on the limitations of your chuck. In our project here, it shouldn't be larger than 65 mm.
3__Turn the side flat to provide for completely round rotation. Now the diameter is about 29 cm.
4__Rechuck the blank and turn it flat at the top side.
5__Carefully inspect the blank again and determine where the opening will be located. In our case the blank is strongly grained on one side but not on the other. The opening should therefore lie on the "weaker" (less beautiful) side. Now you need to mark the new rotational axis on the top and bottom side. A horizontal line starting about 3 cm from the center runs toward the left to the edge, across the side, and again along the bottom toward the center.

6__The center of the opening lies on this level. Now the diameter of the opening needs to be determined.
7__About 15 mm should remain toward the edge, and the opening must include the old center (in this case the screw hole). The diameter of our piece's opening is 150 mm. The new center is marked (C).
   Tip: The distance between the two arrows indicates the diameter of the hole through which the bowl is later hollowed out. In our case the diameter is only 35 mm! For your first attempts, though, you should choose a larger diameter for the opening, and therefore the hole for hollowing out will be larger too.
8__Now mark the center on the bottom as well. It lies on the previously marked line and at the same distance from the edge as the center (C) on the top side.
9__Now affix the blank at the new center between the four-point driver (as large as possible, for example, 38 mm) and the rotating tip.
   Important: Make sure the disc is chucked vertically and that it does not touch the bed of the bank despite its eccentric rotation.

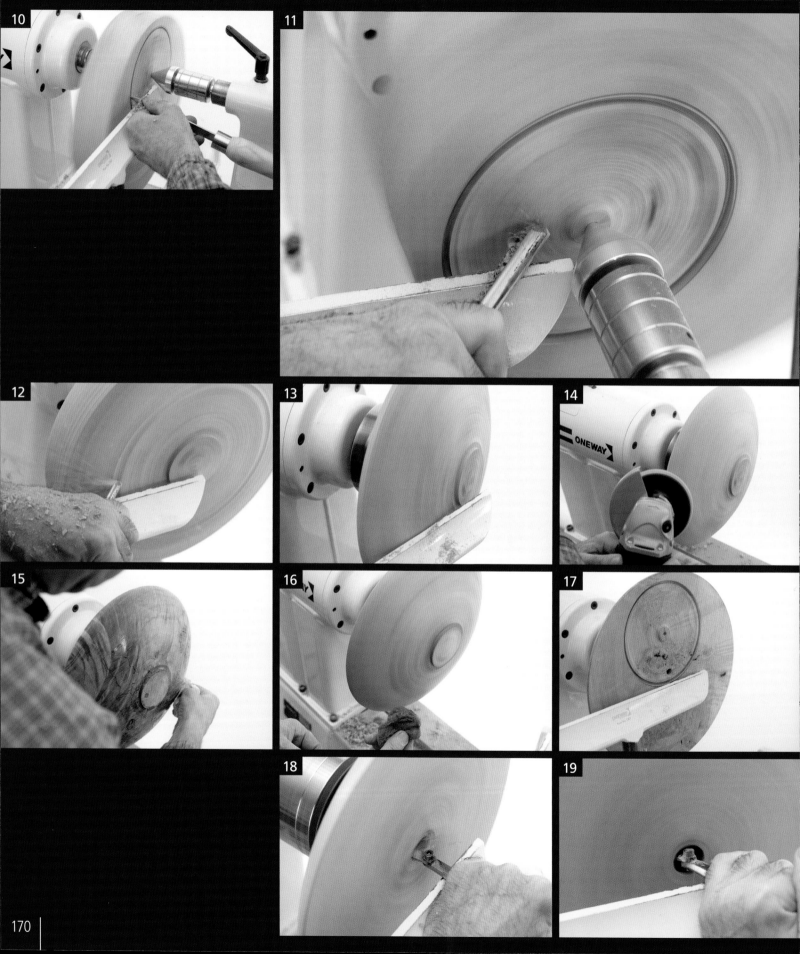

10__Using the parting tool, perforate about 10 mm deep into the new opening . . .

11__ . . . and remove the material of this face to the same depth.

12__Once again, place the blank on the screw and into the chuck to work the bottom side. Do the shaping with the bowl gouge.

13__In Jo's project the bowl won't feature a foot but will rest on a small area.

Tip: You can round off the bottom later when turning the foot. This will result in an interesting swinging bowl.

14__The bottom side is now sanded up to 320 grit with a sanding pad that Jo has affixed to an angle grinder (or use a cordless screwdriver).

Important: Sand in the opposite direction (lathe to the left, sanding pad to the right, or the other way around), but don't allow the lathe or the sanding pad to rotate too quickly.

15__Oil the surface and immediately sand it with a fine-grit abrasive paper (400), or use steel wool (but not if you're using woods that contain tannic agents!).

16__This results in the fine sanding dust mixing with the oil to form a paste that permeates the pores and seals them. The surface gets a smooth and velvety finish.

17__Place the bowl with the foot into the chuck.

Important: Make sure the rotation is completely round and even!

18__Using the woodpecker's beak, a tool developed by Jo, prepare a small opening that will serve to hollow out the bowl. The tool has a straight shaft, and the cutting tip is set vertically toward the front.

19__The maximum diameter of this small opening shows on the rotating piece, via the incision that was made when the blank was chucked between the tips.

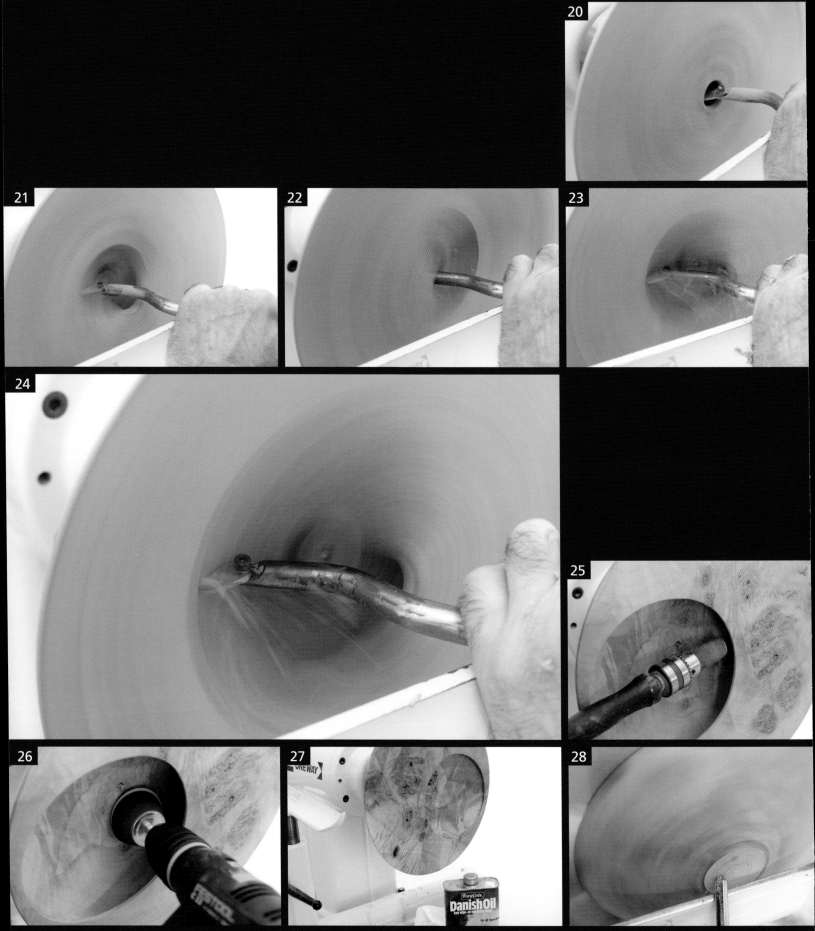

20__Jo's angled tool, the giraffe neck, must be used to hollow out. Here the cutting tip is tilted toward the left.

Important: First make sufficient room for working with the tool into the depth (toward the foot), before widening the cavity.

21__ **22**__ **23**__ **24**__

Very important: When the blank is rotating an increasingly larger opening becomes visible the more the tool advances laterally. The reason: the tool reaches the previously-perforated 10-mm-deep surface of the future bowl opening and creates the breach at this area. But the tool can only be inserted and removed through the small centric hole in the middle, and can only be moved inside of it!

25__Make sure you also get a harmonious curve at the inside. The interior space can be worked with a sanding roller (Kirjes) . . .

26__ . . . or with a sanding pad. The areas that can't be reached need to be sanded by hand.

27__Now oil the surface and immediately sand it as shown on page 171, photo 15.

28__To remove the foot, clamp the bowl onto large aluminum jaws (mega jumbo jaws). The rubber-coated jaws hold the bowl securely without damaging it. This allows for turning off the foot and helps to provide a harmonious curve. Finally, oil the newly-worked surface and immediately sand it, as described before.

Now treat the entire surface with several layers of Danish oil, which enhances the color and the grain. Each layer of oil should dry completely and then be polished—either by hand or with a polishing system, such as the one used for Project 12, *Chinese Sphere,* that's described on page 125.

Cherry
Dia. 10 cm
W 16 cm
H 24 cm

18___DOUBLE-NECK VASE

JO WINTER

Materials	
Tools	Woodpecker's beak
	Bowl gouge
	Parting tool, 1.5 mm
	Parting tool, 3 mm
Wood	Cherry, w. 190 mm, h. 110 mm, l. 270 mm
Accessories	Measuring instruments
	PVC glue
	Glue
	Danish oil

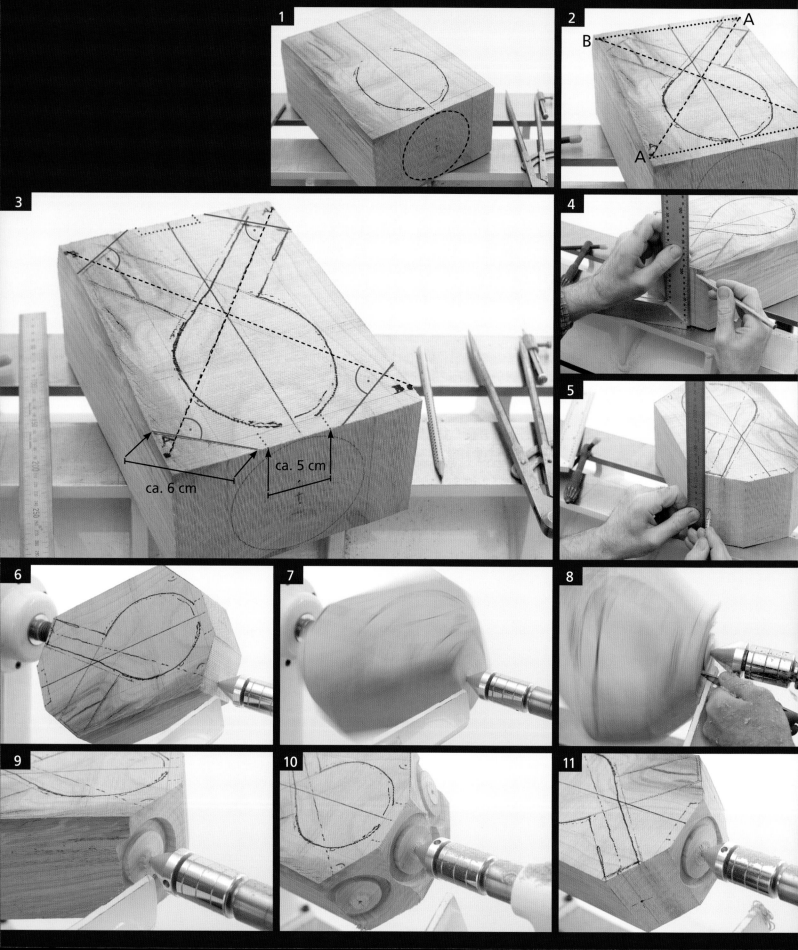

ca. 6 cm

ca. 5 cm

This vase seems inspired by ceramic vessels. The two necks aren't inserted—everything is made from one single piece, and the body of the vase is hollowed out! The vase is turned with several axes. That's why precise planning is essential here, from the choice of the blank, to scribing the basic shape, to the chucking options.

1__Scribe (center first!) the center of the maximum diameter on the end grain wood (mark circle) and the center line. Also draw the outline of the vase body (it should be oval).

2__Mark a line on the surface that is parallel to the narrow edge at a distance of about 1 cm (dotted lines). From the outer points of the line you draw one diagonal each to the opposite line. The two vase necks lie on these diagonals. Mark them on the surface so that the diagonals form the symmetry axes of the necks. The diameter of the neck should be 2 cm.

3__Now mark lines on all four corners of the blank, perpendicular to the diagonal lines A-A and B-B. Later on studs will be turned to these surfaces in order to work the necks. So make sure that the (red) lines for the studs are long enough. In our case, they're about 6 cm. At the same time, mark the position of two additional studs at the top and bottom end of the blank (red dotted lines, width about 5 cm).

4__Saw off the edges along the continuous red lines, and transfer the diagonals to the newly created surfaces.

5__Mark the center of these new lines also. Here the center for the following clamping lies between the tips.

6__Now clamp the blank in the centers of opposite surfaces (A-A) between the driver and the tip so that the future bottom side of the vase lies on the tailstock side (right).

7__Even though the piece is clamped across the diagonals it should now rotate relatively even, since the same amount of material lies on both sides of the axis of rotation. Nevertheless, start with a slow speed and gradually increase it.

8__Turn the stud with the parting tool. Guide the tool past the tailstock and work as perpendicularly as possible to the surface of the stud.

9__Perforate about 10 mm and work the stud back to 5 to 6 mm.

10__Now rechuck the blank and perform the steps from photos 6 to 9 across the diagonal B-B and the center line as well. This way you'll get three studs on the bottom side of the blank.

11__Turn the blank around and clamp it so that the side where the future necks will be located is on the tailstock side. Now add a fourth stud to the top side of the blank—between the necks.

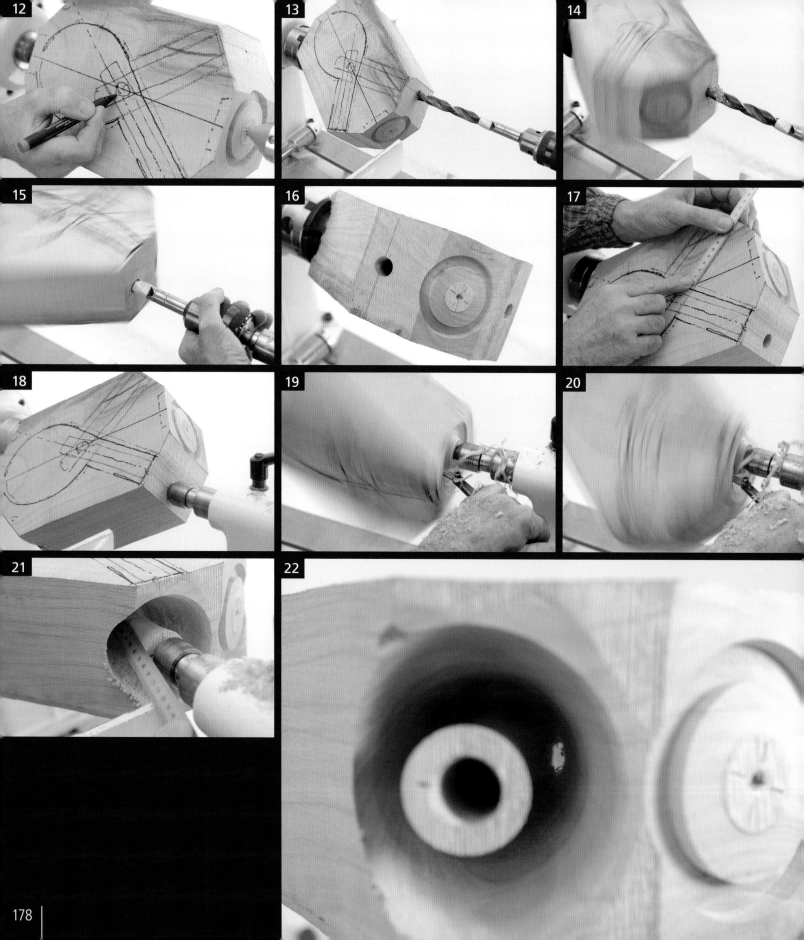

12__Jo shows that the openings of both necks will meet at the center line.

13__Clamp the blank into the chuck, in this case on the stud that was turned to the end of the diagonal B-B.

14__The drill (Douglas or Irwin bit is best) is fitted with the chuck to the tailstock. Mark the drill depth with a piece of tape. Start the lathe slowly, and make sure that the drill has a steady abutment and cuts right away.

15__Continuously pull out the drill bit from the hole to remove slivers and chips. This prevents the drill from getting stuck and producing too much heat.

16__Now rechuck the blank to the stud that lies at the end of the A-A diagonal and repeat the same steps as shown in photos 13 to 15.

17__Measure the length of the necks to determine where they will meet. In our case, the length of the necks is 75 mm.

18__Insert the rotating conical tip into the drill hole to support the blank during the next procedure, that of shaping the neck.

19__Since the workspace is limited due to the tailstock, use the woodpecker's beak.

20__This tool doesn't require much workspace. For our project the shaft can abut vertically. By turning the cutting tip to the left or right it can be used very flexibly.

21__Check the depth (75 mm) and apply only a little pressure with the tailstock so that the thin wall of the neck won't break out. The tailstock should only stabilize it a little.

22__Once the required depth has been reached, rechuck the second drill hole (and the corresponding stud) and work the second neck as described in photos 16 to 21.

Important: The workspace at a depth must be very narrow to avoid catching the wood of the second neck. The diameter of the neck should be even throughout. If you're still unsure you can work alternatingly on both necks. This requires repeated rechucking. Slowly work toward the depth until you reach the meeting point of both necks.

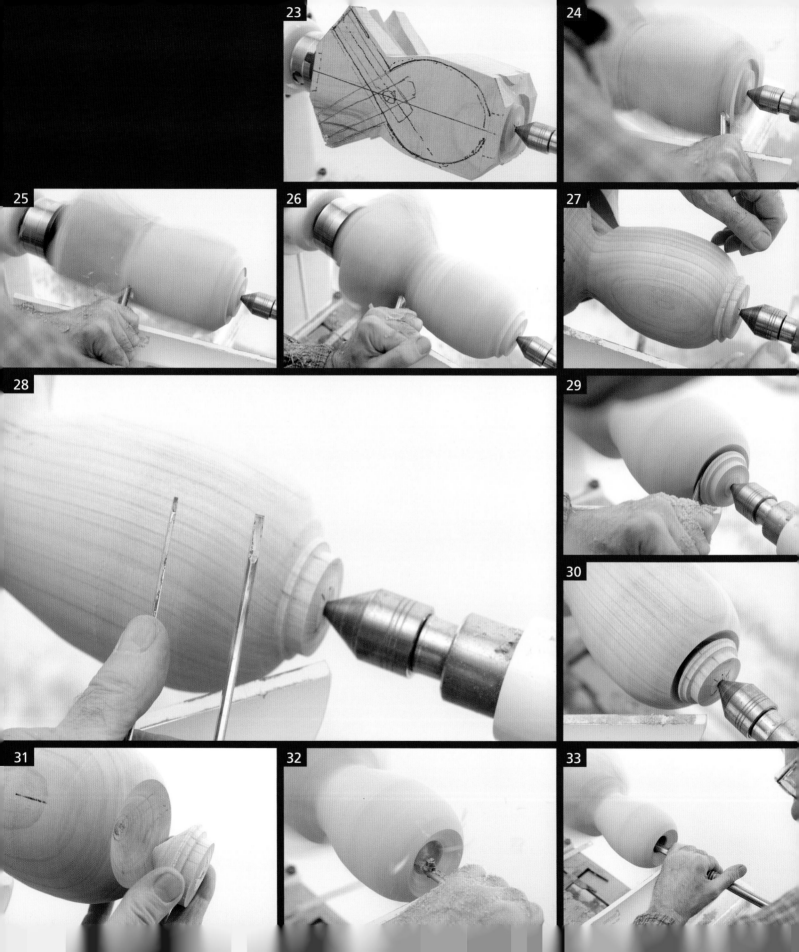

23__When both necks have been finished, saw off the extra wood at both sides of the blank along the marked contour. Clamp the blank onto the stud between the necks and secure the piece with the tailstock.

24__Once it's rechucked, turn the body of the vase.

25__**Important:** Make sure you don't work into the necks. Keep turning off the lathe and control the shape.

26__The bowl gouge or spindle gouge work well for shaping.

27__Check the quality of the surface. If necessary the stud can be downsized to provide a nice curve toward the bottom and to avoid getting a base that's too large.

28__The body of the vase should be hollowed out from the bottom side and later be closed again. To do this you need to cut out a kind of lid from the solid wood. Jo used two parting tools for this task (1.5 mm and 3 mm).

29__First, make an incision with the wide parting tool. The incision should be as narrow as possible, that is, only 3 mm. However, the 3-mm parting tool might get caught at greater depth. So it's only used to work to a depth of 10 to 15 mm.

30__Then, use the narrow parting tool. Contiguous and slightly overlapping cuts make for enough room to not become stuck.

31__Using the narrow parting tool, make an incision, leaving a small stud. The cone can later be broken off manually.

Tip: Before you remove the lid entirely you should add a marking to the lid and the vase. This allows for retracing the grain when the lid is glued in later.

32__Using the woodpecker's beak, hollow out the body of the vase. The cutting tip is affixed onto the oblique end of the shaft so that it hangs slightly downward. This provides for a cutting and not a scraping abutment. To stabilize the piece you might want to use a steady rest.

33__Keep removing the wood chips and slivers from the cavity so there's enough space for the tool. To hollow out the cavity, turn the cutting tip out toward the left. This allows for matching the inner and the outer shape.

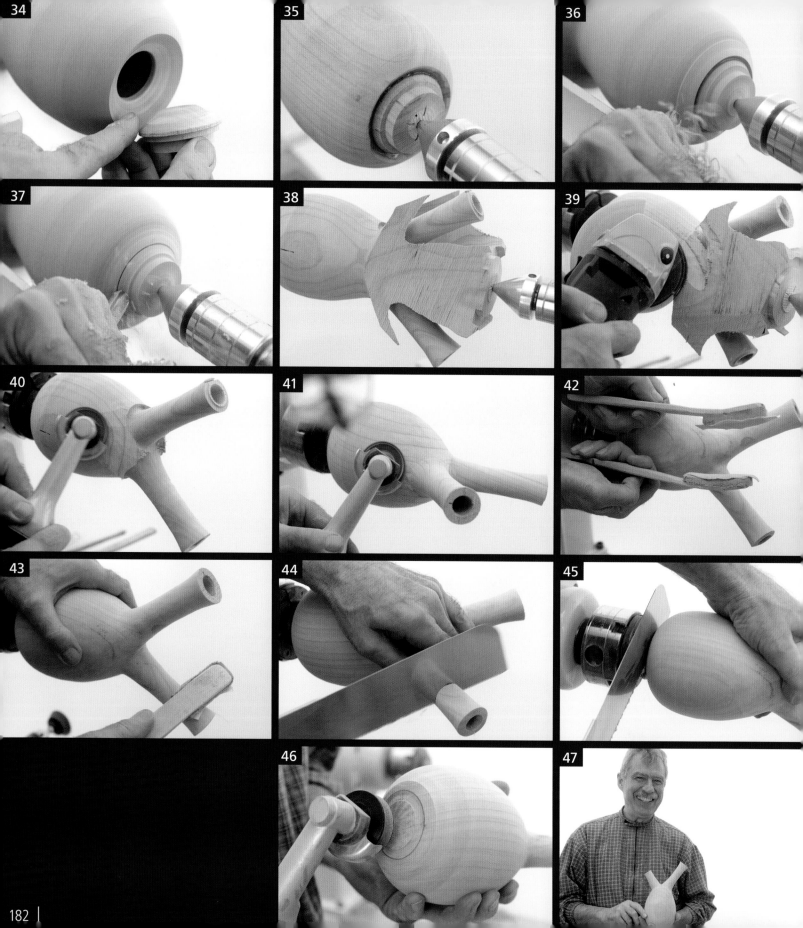

34__Now shorten the cone at the cut-off lid by clamping it into the chuck on the stud and removing the extra material.

Tip: To recognize the point of contact where the lid and the body of the vase will meet, you can press the lid gently against the body of the vase while the lathe is running; at the point of contact the surface is shiny.

35__Using superglue or PVA, glue the lid into the opening.

Important: Match up the direction of the grain!

Tip: Apply pressure with the rotating tip until the glue has dried.

36__Now, create the curve of the vase body.

37__Important: Pull the vase downward until the notch between the curve and the lid disappears and the impact edge lies exactly on the line where the curve of the vase turns into the (concave) bottom surface. This hides the inserted lid.

Tip: If you leave the stud on the lid you can clamp the piece into the chuck for further working.

38__Here the extra material between the two necks can be seen. It's now removed.

39__The angle grinder is well-suited for this task.

Tip: Hold the tool with both hands so it doesn't shift and damage the finished surfaces.

40__Using a small grinder, work out the connection between the necks and the vase body.

41__With a sanding pad mounted on the same tool, match the roundings and equalize the transitions.

42__Jo has made paddles with different curvatures for the final manual work; they feature glued-on foam and a layer of Velcro. He cuts out the matching sanding discs from scraps of larger sanding discs.

43__This allows for sanding the roundings without leaving unsightly surfaces.

44__To provide more visual tension, shorten one of the necks.

45__Saw off the vase at the stud, using a fine Japanese saw . . .

46__ . . . and sand the bottom. Give the vase several layers of oil to emphasize the grain of the cherry wood and to protect it.

47__Heart to heart, Jo presents his finished piece.

GALLERY

HELGA BECKER
Spheres

Olive wood　**Curly maple**　**Curly maple**
Dia. 13 cm　Dia. 16 cm　Dia. 12 cm

HELGA BECKER
Bowl

Curly maple, stained
Dia. 35 cm
H 12 cm

HELGA BECKER
Spindle bowl

Maple, acrylic paint, structured
H 11 cm
L 33.5 cm

HELGA BECKER
Bowl

Curly (European) hornbeam
Dia. 35 cm
H 20.5 cm

HELGA BECKER
Presentation bowl

**Ash, brushed,
blackened**
Dia. 34.5 cm
H 23.5 cm

HELGA BECKER
Presentation bowl

Ash, brushed, blackened
L 52.5 cm
H 6.5 cm

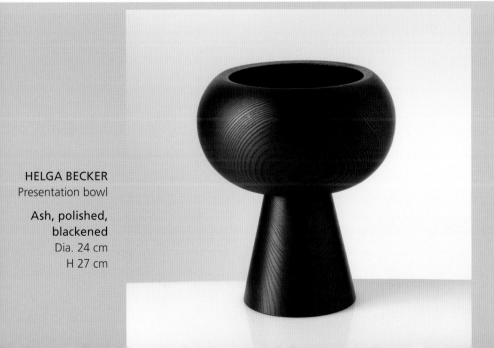

HELGA BECKER
Bowl

Ash, polished, blackened
Dia. 20 cm
H 13 cm

HELGA BECKER
Presentation bowl

**Ash, polished,
blackened**
Dia. 24 cm
H 27 cm

HELGA BECKER
Ways Vases

**Basswood,
shoe polish,
structured**
Dia. 10 cm
H 42 cm

HELGA BECKER
Home Canister

**Basswood,
shoe polish**
Dia. 14 cm
H 12 cm

HELGA BECKER
Home Bowl

**Basswod,
shoe polish**
Dia. 19 cm
H 10 cm

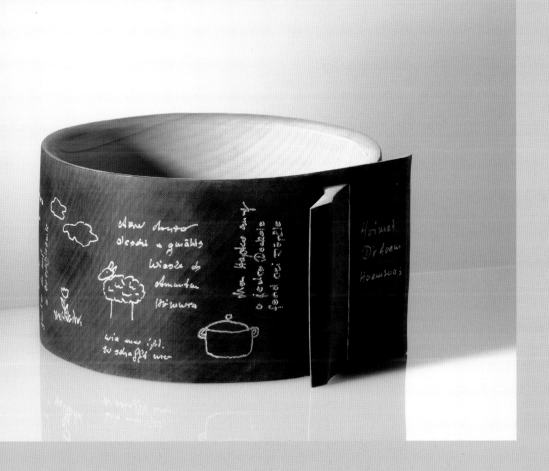

HELGA BECKER
Decorative
spheres

Walnut
Dia. 5 cm
H 10.5 cm

Pear
Dia. 6.5 cm
H 13.5 cm

Maple
Dia. 6 cm
H 12 cm

HELGA BECKER
Presentation bowl

Acacia burl
Dia. 23 cm
H 9 cm

HELGA BECKER
Treasure Canister

**Olive wood,
rosewood**
Dia. 26 cm
H 16 cm

HELGA BECKER
Mother and Child Vases

Cherry, acrylic paint, structured
Dia. 9 cm   Dia. 10.5 cm
H 23 cm   H 35 cm

HELGA BECKER
Us – Them Sculpture

Beech, acrylic paint
H 15 cm – 27 cm

ELI AVISERA
Openwork bowls

Maple, ebony inlays, basswood, and rosewood
Dia. 10 cm   Dia. 8 cm
H 6 cm   H 4.5 cm

ELI AVISERA
Trembleur

Ebony, maple
Dia. 1.5 cm
H 40 cm

ELI AVISERA
Openwork vase

Maple, amaranth, ebony
Dia. 7 cm
H 11 cm

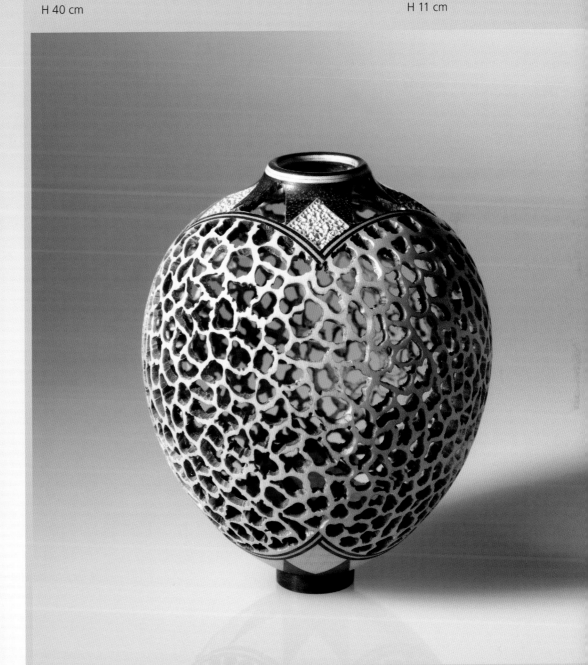

CHRISTIAN DELHON
Object

Elm,
walnut,
ivory,
ebony,
boxwood
Dia. 30 cm
H 50 cm

CHRISTIAN DELHON
Object

Ivory,
ebony,
boxwood
L 20 cm
W 20 cm
H 62 cm

JO WINTER
Triple neck vase

Cherry
Dia. 29 cm
W 18 cm
L 29 cm

ROLAND WALTER
Bowler

Apple
L 30 cm
W 25 cm
H 13 cm

ROLAND WALTER
Cowboy Hats

Various woods
Various sizes

ROLAND WALTER
Top Hat

Ash with colored core
L 32 cm
W 29 cm
H 18 cm

HELGA BECKER is a trained wood-turner and has been running her own woodturning shop since 2000, where she offers courses for beginners and advanced students. She has led work-shops and courses at international symposiums, traveling to countries such as Norway, England, France, Switzerland, and the US. Becker's works are sold in galleries and design shops. She is the author of several books on woodturning, and writes for various national and international woodturning magazines.